D0975522

the GREAT AMERICAN cookbook

the GREAT AMERICAN cookbook

p

This is a Parragon Publishing Book
First published in 2005

Parragon Publishing
Queen Street House
4 Queen Street
Bath BA1 1HE, UK

Copyright © Parragon 2005

Created and produced by THE BRIDGEWATER BOOK COMPANY

Main photographer Emma Neish
Home economist Joy Skipper

ISBN 1-40546-035-0
Printed in Indonesia

NOTE This book uses imperial, metric, and US cup measurements. Follow the same units of measurement throughout; do not mix metric and imperial. All spoon measurements are level: teaspoons are assumed to be 5 ml, and tablespoons are assumed to be 15 ml. Unless otherwise stated, milk is assumed to be whole, eggs and individual vegetables such as carrots are medium, and pepper is freshly ground black pepper.

The times given for each recipe are an approximate guide only. The preparation times may differ according to the techniques used by different people and the cooking times may vary as a result of the type of oven used. Ovens should be preheated to the specified temperature. If using a fan-assisted oven, check the manufacturer's instructions for adjusting the time and temperature.

Recipes using raw eggs should be avoided by infants, the elderly, pregnant women, convalescents, and anyone suffering from an illness. Pregnant and breastfeeding women are advised to avoid eating peanuts and peanut products.

contents

Introduction

This book celebrates the very best in great American home cooking, and takes you on a culinary journey across states and through history, enabling you to experience all the famous tastes of America. Over 100 favorite American recipes have been brought together in this indispensable collection. To make it easier for you to plan your meals and select recipes, all the dishes have been divided into four simple chapters: soups, appetizers, and light meals; main courses; accompaniments; and cakes and desserts.

America is a land of diversity, a melting pot of cultures, and American cooking reflects this huge variety of tastes. Every region offers a whole range of different foods, based on the origins of its people and the foods that they brought with them and that were available to them in the New World. As new immigrants moved from region to region, they were influenced by the land and their neighbors, cooking in their homes what they were eating at local community celebrations, taverns, restaurants, and cafes.

Many foods that are now staples of American cuisine were introduced by the Native American population, who taught the settlers to grow, prepare, and eat corn and also introduced them to pumpkins and cranberries. Even the famous American meal of Thanksgiving Roast Turkey owes its origins to the Native Americans who brought turkeys to the very first Thanksgiving feast in what is now Massachussetts.

The abundant presence of rice in southern cooking is down to the region's suitability for growing rice, and the influence of African-Americans, who brought with them cooking techniques such as smoking, frying, boiling green vegetables, and creating hot and spicy sauces. They also introduced black-eye peas, peanuts, and okra. To this day, a dish of rice with black-eye peas called Hoppin' John is eaten on New Years Day by many southerners for good luck.

Creole and Cajun cooking, famous styles of cooking from Louisiana, were heavily influenced by French settlers, and are often confused. In New Orleans, the French combined the flavors and foods of the Hispanic and African-American locals already living there to create the refined flavours of Creole cuisine. Later on, other French settlers, expelled from what is now Nova Scotia, came to live in the swamps of southwest Louisiana, and created Cajun cuisine, which is heartier and more peppery than Creole, relying on the local game, shrimp and crawfish.

Lone Star Chili is a modern adaptation of a Tex-Mex classic, as are today's tamales, tortillas, chili, and bean dishes. Much of southwest America was once part of Mexico, and local Spanish-American cooking was heavily influenced by native Mexican tastes. More recently, dishes such as Chicken Fajitas, Beef Enchiladas, Chili-Shrimp Tacos, and Pork Tostados owe their existence to the Latin-American influx into cities all across America.

In the Midwest, the German-speaking peoples brought their love of beer and sausage, as well as Sauerbraten, sauerkraut, and dumplings from central Europe. Of course, the most famous European influence found in much American food comes from the huge numbers of Italian immigrants who settled in the great cities, moving from New York to Chicago and westward. After all, where would American food be without pizza, spaghetti, and noodles?

American home cooking has been influenced more by Asian flavors than by Asian recipes, as with the San Francisco wings recipe. Perhaps with so many Chinese restaurants, it has been easier for most Americans to "go out" to dinner! But with recent immigration from other Asian countries, with their own characterful cuisine, Asian cooking shows on television, and more Asian foods in the supermarkets, it is only a matter of time before more varied Asian flavours and recipes become more commonplace.

And so the journey continues. In this book you will find all of these culinary flavors and many more, carefully chosen to give you a true taste of great American cooking.

soups, appetizers, and light meals

George Washington Carver is remembered for founding the 218 Institute in Alabama, in 1881, to educate African-Americans, but he is less well known for his role in the cultivation of peanuts as a cash crop in the 1890s. Peanut soup was one of the recipes he developed to promote the nut's nutritional value.

prepare 10 minutes
cook 25–30 minutes
serves 4–6

creamy tuskegee soup

ingredients

4 tbsp butter
1 small onion, minced
1 celery stalk, minced
1½ tbsp all-purpose flour
3 cups chicken stock
scant ⅔ cup smooth peanut butter
pinch of cayenne pepper
¾ cup light cream
salt and pepper

To garnish

4 tbsp chopped salted peanuts
1 fresh red chili, seeded and
    very finely sliced
2 tbsp thinly sliced celery leaves

did you know?

Now a staple American ingredient, the peanut is originally from Africa, and was introduced to the United States via the slave trade. In the south they are called "goober peas," from the African word nguba, and are primarily grown in Georgia and Virginia.

one Melt the butter in a pan over medium heat. Add the onion and celery and cook, stirring frequently, for 5–8 minutes until they are soft but not brown.

two Sprinkle in the flour and cook, stirring constantly, for an additional 2 minutes. Slowly stir in the stock and bring to a boil, stirring constantly. Add the peanut butter and stir until it "dissolves" and the soup is smooth.

three Reduce the heat to low, add the cayenne pepper and salt and pepper to taste, and let the mixture simmer, half covered, for 20 minutes, stirring occasionally.

four Stir in the cream and heat through, without boiling, for 1–2 minutes. Taste and adjust the seasoning, if necessary.

five Ladle the soup into warmed bowls and sprinkle over the peanuts—they will sink to the bottom, but they won't become soft. Sprinkle over the chili and celery leaves and serve.

This tomato-based Californian soup is brimming with seafood, which can be varied according to availability, and is almost a meal in itself.

prepare 20 minutes
cook 1¼ hours
serves 4–6

cioppino

ingredients

1 lb 2 oz/500 g live mussels
1 lb 2 oz/500 g live clams, rinsed
1¼ cups dry white wine
1 tbsp olive oil
1 large onion, finely chopped
1 celery stalk, finely chopped
1 yellow or green bell pepper, cored, seeded, and finely chopped
1 bay leaf
14 oz/400 g canned chopped tomatoes in juice

3 garlic cloves, minced
1 tbsp tomato paste
1½ cups fish stock or water
6 oz/175 g small squid, cleaned and cut into small pieces
8 oz/225 g skinless white fish fillets, such as cod, sole, or haddock
5½ oz/150 g small scallops, or cooked shelled shrimp
chopped fresh parsley, to garnish

one Discard any broken mussels and those with open shells that do not close when tapped. Rinse, pull off any "beards," and if there are barnacles, scrape them off with a knife under cold running water. Put the mussels in a large heavy-bottom pan. Cover tightly and cook over high heat for 4 minutes, or until the mussels open, shaking the pan occasionally. Discard any mussels that remain closed.

two When cool enough to handle, remove the mussels from the shells, adding any additional juices to the cooking liquid. Strain the cooking liquid through a muslin-lined sieve and reserve.

three Put the clams into a heavy pan with ¼ cup of the wine. Cover tightly, place over medium-high heat, and cook for 2–4 minutes until they open. Remove the clams from the shells and strain the cooking liquid through a muslin-lined sieve and reserve.

four Heat the olive oil in a large pan over medium-low heat. Add the onion, celery, and bell pepper and cook for 3–4 minutes until the onion softens, stirring occasionally. Add the remaining wine, bay leaf, tomatoes, garlic, and tomato paste. Continue cooking for 10 minutes.

five Stir in the fish stock, squid, and reserved mussel and clam cooking liquids. Bring to a boil, reduce the heat, and simmer for 35–40 minutes until the vegetables and squid are tender.

six Add the fish, mussels, and clams and simmer, stirring occasionally, for 4 minutes, or until the fish becomes opaque. Stir in the scallops and continue simmering for 3–4 minutes until heated through. Remove the bay leaf, ladle the soup into warm bowls, and sprinkle with chopped parsley.

The richness of this tasty chilled soup is balanced by the sharp injection of lime and Tabasco. An optional dash of tequila adds an extra southwestern kick to the dish. This is the perfect appetizer for an alfresco lunch or dinner southern style. Follow with Barbecue Rack of Ribs. A pitcher of sangria would complete the summery scene.

prepare 15 minutes,
plus 2 hours' chilling
cook no cooking
serves 4

chilled avocado and cilantro soup

ingredients

4 ripe avocados

1 shallot or 2 scallions, finely chopped

3½ cups chicken or strongly flavored
 vegetable stock

⅔ cup sour cream, plus extra
 to serve

2 tbsp tomato paste

few drops of Tabasco sauce, or to taste

juice of 1 lime, or to taste

1 tbsp tequila (optional)

1 tbsp chopped fresh cilantro, plus extra
 to garnish

salt and pepper

Flour Tortillas, to serve

one Cut each avocado in half lengthwise and twist the 2 halves in opposite directions to separate. Stab the pit of each avocado with the point of a sharp knife and lift out.

two Peel, then coarsely chop the avocado halves and place in a food processor or blender with the shallot, stock, sour cream, tomato paste, Tabasco, lime juice, tequila (if using), chopped cilantro, and salt and pepper to taste. Process until smooth, then taste and add more Tabasco, lime juice, and salt and pepper if necessary.

three Transfer the mixture to a large bowl, cover, and let chill in the refrigerator for at least 2 hours, or until thoroughly chilled.

four Divide the soup between 4 chilled serving bowls and serve, topped with a spoonful of sour cream, garnished with extra chopped cilantro, and accompanied by some Flour Tortillas.

Stoke up your energy reserves with a bowl of this hearty soup—both comforting and sustaining. It is highly economical as well as quick and easy to prepare.

prepare 20 minutes
cook 35 minutes
serves 4

beef and pea soup

ingredients

2 tbsp vegetable oil

1 large onion, finely chopped

2 garlic cloves, finely chopped

1 green bell pepper, cored, seeded, and sliced

2 carrots, sliced

14 oz/400 g canned black-eye peas

1 cup freshly ground beef

1 tsp each ground cumin, chili powder, and paprika

¼ cabbage, sliced

8 oz/225 g tomatoes, peeled and chopped

2½ cups beef stock

salt and pepper

To serve

tortilla chips, warmed corn tortillas, or Flour Tortillas

one Heat the oil in a large pan over medium heat. Add the onion and garlic and cook, stirring frequently, for 5 minutes, or until softened. Add the bell pepper and carrots and cook for an additional 5 minutes.

two Meanwhile, drain the peas, reserving the liquid from the can. Place two-thirds of the peas, reserving the remainder, in a food processor or blender with the pea liquid and process until smooth.

three Add the ground beef to the pan and cook, stirring constantly, to break up any lumps, until well browned. Add the spices and cook, stirring, for 2 minutes. Add the cabbage, tomatoes, stock, and puréed peas and season to taste with salt and pepper. Bring to a boil, then reduce the heat, cover, and let simmer for 15 minutes, or until the vegetables are tender.

four Stir in the reserved peas, cover, and let simmer for an additional 5 minutes. Ladle the soup into four warmed soup bowls and serve with a bowl of tortilla chips or some warmed corn tortillas. Alternatively, devotees of southwestern cuisine may like to make a batch of homemade Flour Tortillas as an accompaniment.

Chowders are thick soups that have milk and potatoes as their main
ingredients, to which other flavors are added. This is a classic version
from New England, flavored with fresh clams.

prepare 15 minutes
cook 30 minutes
serves 4

new england clam chowder

ingredients

2 lb/900 g live clams

4 bacon strips, chopped

2 tbsp butter

1 onion, chopped

1 tbsp chopped fresh thyme

1 large potato, diced

1¼ cups milk

1 bay leaf

1⅔ cups heavy cream

1 tbsp chopped fresh parsley

salt and pepper

one Scrub the clams and put them into a large pan with a splash of water. Cook over high
heat for 3–4 minutes until they open. Discard any that remain closed. Strain, reserving the
cooking liquid. Set aside until cool enough to handle, reserving 8 for a garnish.

two Remove the clams from their shells, chopping them roughly if large, and set aside.

three In a clean pan, fry the bacon until browned and crisp. Drain on paper towels. Add
the butter to the same pan, and when it has melted, add the onion. Pan-fry for 4–5 minutes
until soft but not colored. Add the thyme and cook briefly before adding the diced potato,
reserved clam cooking liquid, milk, and bay leaf. Bring to a boil and simmer for 10 minutes,
or until the potato is just tender.

four Discard the bay leaf, then transfer to a food processor and blend until smooth,
or push through a strainer into a bowl.

five Add the clams, bacon, and cream. Simmer for another 2–3 minutes until heated
through. Season to taste with salt and pepper. Stir in the chopped parsley and serve,
garnished with the reserved clams in their shells.

cook's tip

The smart way to present this dish
is to sit 2 of the reserved clams in
their shells on top of each bowl of
soup before serving.

Mango, although lusciously fruity, goes wonderfully well with savory ingredients and is enhanced, not masked, by robust flavorings. The color of its succulent flesh is an added bonus.

prepare 15 minutes, plus 2 hours' chilling
cook no cooking
serves 4

shrimp and mango cocktail

ingredients

6 cherry tomatoes

1 large ripe mango

1 fresh mild green chili, seeded and finely chopped

juice of 1 lime

1 tbsp chopped fresh cilantro, plus extra to garnish

14 oz/400 g shelled cooked jumbo shrimp

salt and pepper

one Place the tomatoes in a heatproof bowl and pour over enough boiling water to cover. Let stand for 1–2 minutes, then remove the tomatoes with a slotted spoon, peel off the skins, and refresh in cold water. Dice the flesh and place in a large, nonmetallic bowl.

two Slice the mango lengthwise on either side of the flat central seed. Peel the 2 mango pieces and cut the flesh into chunks. Slice and peel any remaining flesh around the seed, then cut into chunks. Add to the tomatoes with any juice.

three Add the chili, lime juice, chopped cilantro, and salt and pepper to taste. Cover and let chill in the refrigerator for 2 hours to allow the flavors to develop.

four Remove the dish from the refrigerator. Fold the shrimp gently into the mango mixture and divide between 4 serving dishes. Garnish with chopped cilantro and serve immediately.

While northerners shiver through the cold winter months and comfort themselves with warming stews and casseroles, Floridians feast on fresh fruit salads. The use of fresh lime and chili gives this example a Latino flavor from Miami.

prepare 15 minutes, plus 1 hour's chilling
cook no cooking
serves 4

florida fruit cocktail

ingredients

1 large ripe mango
2 large oranges
1 pink grapefruit
1 tsp finely grated lime rind
4 tbsp fresh lime juice, or to taste
1 fresh red chili, seeded and finely sliced
4 tbsp grated fresh coconut, or moist shredded coconut
chopped fresh cilantro, to garnish

variations

This is a mix and match salad that is equally good with whatever fresh tropical fruit is available — try pineapple, carambola, papaya, and even avocado. It's a refreshing first course as it is, but for a more substantial dish, add poached shrimp or crabmeat, or serve with cottage cheese

one To prepare the mango, slice it lengthwise on either side of the flat central seed. Peel the 2 mango pieces and cut the flesh into chunks. Slice and peel any remaining flesh around the seed, then cut into chunks and put into a nonmetallic bowl.

two Peel the oranges and grapefruit, carefully removing all the bitter white pith. As each fruit is peeled, separate it into segments over the bowl, cutting between the membranes and letting the segments drop into the bowl. Squeeze the juice from the membranes into the bowl.

three Stir the lime rind, lime juice, chili, and coconut into the bowl. Cover and let chill for at least 1 hour to let the flavors blend.

four Stir the fruit salad and add extra lime juice, if necessary. Spoon into four bowls and sprinkle with fresh cilantro to serve.

This elegant appetizer couldn't be simpler to make but requires several hours' chilling for the raw fish to "cook" in the lime juice—you can tell that it's done because the fish turns opaque.

prepare 20 minutes, plus 8 hours' chilling
cook no cooking
serves 4

ceviche salad

ingredients

1 lb/450 g salmon, red snapper, or sole fillets, skinned

1 small onion, finely chopped

1 fresh jalapeño chili or 2 small fresh mild green chilies, seeded and finely chopped

juice of 3 limes

1 tbsp extra virgin olive oil

1 tbsp chopped fresh cilantro, plus extra to garnish

1 tbsp snipped fresh chives or dill

1 ripe avocado

2 tomatoes, peeled and diced

2 tbsp capers, rinsed (optional)

salt and pepper

one Skin the fish and cut it into strips or slices. Place the fish, onion, chili, lime juice, oil, and herbs in a nonmetallic dish and mix together. Cover and let chill in the refrigerator for 8 hours or overnight, stirring occasionally to ensure that the fish is well coated in the marinade.

two When ready to serve, remove the dish from the refrigerator and season to taste with salt and pepper.

three Cut the avocado in half lengthwise and twist the 2 halves in opposite directions to separate. Stab the pit with the point of a sharp knife and lift out of the avocado. Peel then thinly slice the avocado halves. Arrange the fish mixture on a large serving plate with the tomatoes and avocado. Sprinkle the capers over the mixture (if using), and sprinkle with chopped cilantro to garnish.

note

People with certain diseases (such as diabetes or liver disease) or weakened immune systems should never eat raw fish. The elderly and pregnant women (along with nursing mothers and young children) should also avoid eating raw fish.

This salad is traditionally a combination of celery, apples, and walnuts, dressed with mayonnaise. Here, with the addition of sliced steak, it is turned into a light lunch or supper dish.

prepare 15 minutes
cook 6–10 minutes
serves 4

steak waldorf salad

ingredients

2 tenderloin steaks, about 6 oz/175 g each
  and 1-inch/2.5-cm thick
olive or sunflower-seed oil, for brushing
1 tbsp whole grain mustard
⅔ cup mayonnaise
1 tbsp lemon juice

1 lb 2 oz/500 g eating apples
4 celery stalks, thinly sliced
generous ⅜ cup walnut halves,
  broken into pieces
3½ oz/100 g mixed salad greens
pepper

one Heat a thick, cast-iron stove-top pan or heavy-bottom skillet over medium heat. Brush each steak with oil and season to taste with pepper. When hot, add the steaks to the pan, and cook for 6–7 minutes for rare or 8–10 minutes for medium, turning the steaks frequently and brushing once or twice with oil. Remove from the pan and set aside.

two Meanwhile, stir the mustard into the mayonnaise. Put the lemon juice into a large bowl. Peel and core the apples, then cut them into small chunks and immediately toss them in the lemon juice. Stir in the mustard mayonnaise. Add the celery and walnuts to the apples and toss together.

three Arrange the salad greens on 4 plates, then divide the apple mixture between them. Very thinly slice the steaks, arrange on top of the salad, and serve immediately.

did you know?

Waldorf salad is named after the prestigious Waldorf Astoria Hotel in New York, as it was here that the dish originated at the end of the 19th century

This New Orleans classic of poached shrimp with piquant rusty-red sauce was first served at Arnaud's, one of the city's oldest restaurants. This is the restaurant's own recipe.

prepare 15 minutes,
plus 45 minutes' chilling
cook 5–8 minutes
serves 4–6

shrimp rémoulade

ingredients

1 ½ tbsp salt
1 lemon, sliced
1 lb 12 oz/800 g large unshelled raw
  shrimp

Rémoulade sauce
2 oz/55 g scallions, coarsely chopped
2 oz/55 g celery stalks, coarsely chopped
1 large garlic clove
4 tbsp chopped fresh parsley
2 tbsp Creole mustard or German mustard
2 tbsp superfine sugar
2 tbsp cider vinegar or tomato ketchup

1 ½ tbsp prepared horseradish
1 tbsp paprika
½ tsp cayenne pepper
½ tsp salt
¼ tsp ground black pepper
few drops of hot pepper sauce, to taste
about ⅔ cup corn or peanut oil

To serve
shredded iceberg lettuce
2 hard-cooked eggs, shelled and sliced
2 tomatoes, sliced

did you know?

One of the characteristics of Creole recipes is to include French words in the titles, such as "rémoulade," even if there is little similarity with the traditional French version. Anyone expecting this sauce to taste like its creamy mustard-flavored cousin will be surprised—this rémoulade sauce is much spicier.

one To make the sauce, put the scallions, celery, garlic, and parsley into a food processor and pulse until finely chopped. Add the mustard, sugar, vinegar, horseradish, paprika, cayenne pepper, salt, pepper, and hot pepper sauce to taste and whiz until well blended. With the motor running, slowly pour in the oil through the feed tube in a slow, steady stream until a thick, creamy sauce forms. Transfer to a large bowl, cover, and set aside.

two To poach the shrimp, bring a large pan of water with the salt and lemon slices to a boil over high heat. Add the shrimp and cook just until they turn pink.

three Drain the shrimp well and put them under cold running water until completely chilled. Shell and devein them, adding them to the sauce as you go. Stir together, then cover and let chill for at least 45 minutes, but ideally overnight. Serve on a bed of lettuce with hard-cooked eggs and sliced tomatoes.

The original recipe for this baked oyster dish is a guarded secret of Antoine's, New Orleans' oldest Creole restaurant, but many versions have been created. Spinach features in most.

oysters rockefeller

ingredients

24 large live oysters
rock salt
3 tbsp butter
6 scallions, chopped
1 large garlic clove, crushed
3 tbsp finely chopped celery
1½ oz/40 g watercress sprigs

1¾ cups young spinach leaves, rinsed
  and any tough stems removed
1 tbsp aniseed-flavored liqueur
4 tbsp fresh bread crumbs
few drops of hot pepper sauce, to taste
salt and pepper
lemon wedges, to serve

one Preheat the oven to 400°F/200°C. Shuck the oysters, running an oyster knife under each oyster to loosen it from its shell. Pour off the liquor. Arrange a ½–¾-inch/1–2-cm layer of salt in a roasting pan large enough to hold the oysters in a single layer, or use 2 roasting pans. Nestle the oyster shells in the salt so that they remain upright. Cover with a thick, damp dish towel and let chill while you make the topping.

two If you don't have oyster plates with indentations that hold the shells upright, line 4 plates with a layer of salt deep enough to hold six shells upright. Set the plates aside.

three Melt half the butter in a large skillet over medium heat. Add the scallions, garlic, and celery and cook, stirring frequently, for 2–3 minutes until softened.

four Stir in the remaining butter, then add the watercress and spinach and cook, stirring constantly, for 1 minute, or until the leaves wilt. Transfer to a blender or small food processor and add the liqueur, bread crumbs, hot pepper sauce, and salt and pepper to taste. Whiz until well blended.

five Spoon 2–3 teaspoons of the sauce over each oyster. Bake in the oven for 20 minutes. Transfer to the prepared plates and serve with lemon wedges.

cook's tip

The exact amount of sauce needed depends on the size of the oysters—this is enough to top 24 large oysters. Any leftovers can be stirred into vegetable soups, or mixed with mayonnaise to make a sauce for sandwiches.

Because of the laborious work involved in extracting the meat from crabs, fresh crabmeat is relatively expensive. A dip is one way to stretch the flavor, although hosts should be aware that guests will rate the party-giver on the amount of crab in the dip—the more the better.

prepare 10 minutes,
plus 24 hours' optional chilling
cook 15 minutes
serves 8–12

warm crab dip

ingredients

1¾ cups cream cheese
3 oz/85 g medium Cheddar cheese, grated
1 cup sour cream
4 tbsp mayonnaise
2 tbsp freshly squeezed lemon juice,
 or to taste
2 tsp Dijon mustard
2 tsp Worcestershire sauce, plus extra
 to taste

1 lb 2 oz/500 g cooked fresh crabmeat,
 picked over, or thawed and patted
 dry if frozen
1 garlic clove, cut in half
butter, for greasing
salt and pepper
fresh dill sprigs, to garnish
savory crackers, to serve

did you know?

Family recipes for crab dip pass from mother to daughter in the south, along with the family chafing dish, which is ideal for keeping this rich dip warm while guests mingle. Sesame seed crackers, called benne wafers, are the traditional southern accompaniment, but any small savory cracker is fine.

one This dip tastes best if all the ingredients are mixed together 24 hours in advance to let the flavors develop, but it still tastes good if made just before serving. Put the cream cheese into a bowl and stir in the Cheddar cheese, sour cream, mayonnaise, lemon juice, mustard, and Worcestershire sauce.

two Add the crabmeat and salt and pepper to taste and gently stir together. Taste and add extra Worcestershire sauce, if desired. Cover and let chill for up to 24 hours.

three When you are ready to heat the dip, remove it from the refrigerator and let it come to room temperature. Meanwhile, preheat the oven to 350°F/180°C. Rub the cut sides of the garlic clove over the base and sides of an ovenproof dish suitable for serving from (see Step 4), then lightly grease. Spoon the crab mixture into the dish and smooth the surface. Heat the dip through in the oven for 15 minutes.

four This dip is best kept warm when served, traditionally by using a chafing dish heated by a candle. Either spoon the dip into such a dish, sprinkle with dill, and set over the heat source, or set the dip in its ovenproof dish over a fondue burner and garnish with dill. Serve with savory crackers.

Fried oysters are one of the most traditional fillings of this New Orleans classic. Once you choose your filling, you just have to decide if you want it "undressed" (plain) or "dressed" (with lettuce, tomatoes, and mayonnaise), as in this recipe.

prepare 25 minutes
cook 10 minutes
serves 4

oyster po' boys

ingredients

generous ¼ cup yellow cornmeal
½ cup all-purpose flour
pinch of cayenne pepper
24 fresh live oysters
vegetable oil, for deep-frying
1 French baguette
hot pepper sauce, to taste (optional)
2 dill pickles, sliced (optional)
mayonnaise
4 tomatoes, sliced
shredded iceberg lettuce
salt and pepper

did you know?

The "po' boy" name supposedly came about in 1929 when two New Orleans restaurateurs took pity on striking streetcar workers and offered the "poor boys" sandwiches made from the day's leftovers. It is also nicknamed a "peacemaker" because husbands traditionally bring one home to end a marital spat.

one Put the cornmeal, flour, cayenne pepper, and salt and pepper to taste into a plastic bag, hold closed, and shake to mix. Shuck the oysters, running an oyster knife under each oyster to loosen it from its shell. Pour off the liquor. Add the oysters to the bag and shake until well coated.

two Heat at least 2 inches/5 cm of oil in the largest skillet you have over high heat until the temperature reaches 350–375°F/180–190°C, or until a cube of bread browns in 30 seconds. Add as many oysters as will fit without overcrowding and fry for 2–3 minutes until the coating is crisp and lightly browned. Remove the oysters from the oil with a slotted spoon and drain on paper towels. Reheat the oil, then cook the remaining oysters.

three Cut the baguette in half, without cutting all the way through. Open the bread out like a book and use a spoon to scoop out the crumbs from the bottom half, leaving a border all around the edge.

four Spread mayonnaise over the top and bottom halves. Lay the oysters all along the length. Sprinkle with hot pepper sauce to taste and dill pickles, if using. Dress with tomato slices all along the length, then add the shredded lettuce. Close the sandwich and cut into 4 equal portions and wrap in paper napkins to serve.

The steak in this recipe should be cut into very thin slices, so it is partially frozen beforehand to make this easier to do. Put the steak in the freezer for about 2 hours before you need it.

prepare 15 minutes, plus 2 hours' freezing
cook 15–22 minutes
serves 4

philly cheesesteak sandwiches

ingredients

1 French baguette
12 oz/350 g boneless rib-eye steak, partially frozen
3 tbsp olive oil
1 onion, thinly sliced

1 green bell pepper, cored, seeded, and thinly sliced
2¾ oz/75 g provolone or mozzarella cheese, thinly sliced
salt and pepper
hot pepper sauce, to serve

one Cut the baguette into 4 equal lengths, then cut each piece in half horizontally. Thinly slice the partially frozen steak across the grain.

two Heat 2 tablespoons of the oil in a large skillet over medium heat, add the onion and bell pepper, and cook, stirring occasionally, for 10–15 minutes until both vegetables are softened and the onion is golden brown. Push the mixture to one side of the skillet.

three Heat the remaining oil in the skillet over medium heat. When hot, add the steak and stir-fry for 4–5 minutes until tender. Stir the onion mixture and steak together and season to taste with salt and pepper.

four Preheat the broiler to medium. Divide the steak mixture between the 4 bottom halves of bread and top with the cheese. Place them on a broiler rack and broil for 1–2 minutes until the cheese has melted, then cover with the top halves of bread and press down gently. Serve immediately with hot pepper sauce.

did you know?

This sandwich dates back to 1930, when it was dreamed up by the Italian community in south Philadelphia. It can also be made with chicken. They say that you cannot make a true Philly Cheesesteak Sandwich outside Philadelphia, as the authentic variety of bread roll is unavailable elsewhere. This recipe uses a baguette as a compromise.

There aren't many Americans who don't remember these aptly named sandwiches from their childhood—a flavorsome, all-American favorite. In fact, they can be too sloppy to pick up easily, so you may need to use a knife and fork.

prepare 10 minutes
cook 25 minutes
serves 4

sloppy joes

ingredients

1 tbsp sunflower-seed or corn oil
1 onion, finely chopped
1 red bell pepper, cored, seeded, and finely chopped
1 lb/450 g freshly ground beef
1 tbsp all-purpose flour
½ tsp dried thyme

1¼ cups canned condensed cream of tomato soup
½ cup water
½ tbsp Worcestershire sauce, or to taste
4 sesame seed buns
salt and pepper
potato chips, to serve

one Heat the oil in a large skillet or pan over medium-high heat. Add the onion and bell pepper and cook, stirring frequently, for 5–8 minutes until soft but not browned. Add the beef and cook, stirring constantly and breaking up the meat with a wooden spoon, until no pinkness remains.

two Sprinkle in the flour and thyme and cook, stirring constantly, for a further 2 minutes.

three Stir in the soup, water, Worcestershire sauce, and salt and pepper to taste. Bring to a boil, then reduce the heat and simmer, stirring occasionally, for 15 minutes, or until the mixture thickens and the beef is cooked through.

four Put the bottom half of each bun on an individual serving plate. Spoon over the Sloppy Joe mixture and replace the top halves. Serve with potato chips on the side.

cook's tip

These are always served hot, but the Sloppy Joe mixture can be made in advance and reheated. It's worth making double the quantity and freezing the second amount—it can be kept for up to three months.

Introduced by the Italians and packed with delicious Italian ingredients, this recipe features a Bolognese sauce. Wrap the sandwiches in foil for transporting and supply lots of paper napkins for catching the juices!

prepare 15 minutes, plus 1 hour's standing
cook 20–25 minutes
serves 4

italian steak heroes

ingredients

1 tbsp olive oil
1 small onion, finely chopped
1 garlic clove, finely chopped
1 small red bell pepper, cored, seeded, and finely chopped
3½ oz/100 g white mushrooms, finely chopped
⅞ cup freshly ground steak
½ cup red wine
2 tbsp tomato paste
4 ciabatta rolls
extra virgin olive oil, for brushing
2¾ oz/75 g mozzarella cheese
2 tbsp torn fresh basil leaves
salt and pepper

did you know?

This classic sandwich comes under a variety of labels—the hoagie, the submarine, the bomber, the grinder, the wedge, and the zep, to name a few!

one Heat the olive oil in a large pan over medium heat, add the onion, garlic, bell pepper, and mushrooms, and cook, stirring occasionally, for 5–10 minutes until softened and beginning to brown.

two Add the ground steak and cook, stirring frequently and breaking up any lumps with a wooden spoon, for 5 minutes, or until browned on all sides. Add the wine, tomato paste, and salt and pepper to taste and let simmer for 10 minutes, stirring occasionally. Remove from the heat.

three Split the bread rolls in half and brush both halves with extra virgin olive oil. Put the bottom halves onto a piece of foil and spoon an equal quantity of the sauce on top of each.

four Slice the cheese, then divide between the roll bottoms and arrange on top of the sauce. Add the basil leaves and cover with the tops of the rolls. Press down gently and wrap in the foil. Leave the sandwiches for at least 1 hour before serving.

The quesadilla is the southwestern take on a toasted cheese sandwich. Oaxacan cheese, also known as Asadero cheese, is the strictly authentic cheese to use, but mozzarella makes a good alternative.

prepare 15 minutes
cook 32–40 minutes
serves 4

chorizo and cheese quesadillas

ingredients

4 oz/115 g mozzarella cheese, grated

4 oz/115 g Cheddar cheese, grated

8 oz/225 g cooked chorizo sausage (outer casing removed) or ham, diced

4 scallions, finely chopped

2 fresh green chilies, such as poblano, seeded and finely chopped

8 Flour Tortillas

vegetable oil, for brushing

salt and pepper

lime wedges, to garnish

To serve

Guacamole

Pico de Gallo Salsa

one Place the cheeses, chorizo, scallions, chilies, and salt and pepper to taste in a bowl and mix together.

two Divide the mixture between 4 of the Flour Tortillas, then top with the remaining tortillas.

three Brush a large, nonstick or heavy-bottom skillet with oil and heat over medium heat. Add 1 quesadilla and cook, pressing it down with a spatula, for 4–5 minutes until the underside is crisp and lightly browned. Turn over and cook the other side until the cheese is melting. Remove from the skillet and keep warm. Cook the remaining quesadillas.

four Cut each quesadilla into quarters, arrange on a warmed serving plate, and serve, garnished with lime wedges and accompanied by some Guacamole and Pico de Gallo Salsa.

Who can resist diving into a molten mountain of nachos and biting into that great combination of the soggy, chewy, and crispy? Nachos are so easy to prepare, especially if you use canned refried beans. They are delicious with an icy glass of tequila.

prepare 10 minutes
cook 5–8 minutes
serves 6

nachos

ingredients

6 oz/175 g tortilla chips
1 quantity Refried Beans or 14 oz/400 g
   canned refried beans, warmed
2 tbsp finely chopped bottled jalapeño
   chilies
7 oz/200 g canned or bottled pimientos
   or roasted bell peppers, drained and
   finely sliced
4 oz/115 g Gruyère cheese, grated
4 oz/115 g Cheddar cheese, grated
salt and pepper

To serve
Guacamole
sour cream

one Preheat the oven to 400°F/200°C.

two Spread the tortilla chips out over the bottom of a large, shallow ovenproof dish or roasting pan. Cover with the Refried Beans. Sprinkle over the chilies and pimientos and season to taste with salt and pepper. Mix the cheeses together in a bowl and sprinkle on top.

three Bake in the oven for 5–8 minutes until the cheese is bubbling and melted. Serve immediately with some Guacamole and sour cream.

This is another southwestern delight. Replace the ground pork with beef if you prefer and, to save time, use corn chips or nacho chips instead of the cooked tortilla wedges. Enjoy these tostadas with a margarita for a memorable "happy hour."

pork tostadas

ingredients

1 tbsp vegetable oil, plus extra
  for the tortillas
1 small onion, finely chopped
2 garlic cloves, finely chopped
1 lb/450 g freshly ground pork
2 tsp ground cumin
2 tsp chili powder, plus extra to garnish
1 tsp ground cinnamon
6 soft corn tortillas, cut into wedges
shredded iceberg lettuce
sour cream
red bell pepper, cored, seeded,
  and finely diced
salt and pepper
Pico de Gallo Salsa (optional), to serve

Taco sauce (optional)
1 tbsp olive oil
1 onion, finely chopped
1 green bell pepper, seeded and diced
1–2 fresh hot green chilies, such as
  jalapeño, seeded and finely chopped
3 garlic cloves, crushed
1 tsp ground cumin
1 tsp ground coriander
1 tsp brown sugar
1 lb/450 g ripe tomatoes, peeled and
  coarsely chopped
juice of ½ lemon
salt and pepper

one To make the Taco Sauce, if using, heat the oil in a deep skillet over medium heat. Add the onion and cook for 5 minutes, or until softened. Add the bell pepper and chilies and cook for 5 minutes. Add the garlic, cumin, coriander, and sugar and cook the sauce for an additional 2 minutes, stirring. Add the tomatoes, lemon juice, and salt and pepper to taste. Bring to a boil, then reduce the heat and let simmer for 10 minutes. Remove from the heat and set aside.

two Heat 1 tablespoon of oil in a heavy-bottom skillet over medium heat. Add the onion and garlic and cook, stirring frequently, for 5 minutes, or until softened. Increase the heat, add the ground pork, and cook, stirring constantly to break up any lumps, until well browned.

three Add the cumin, chili powder, cinnamon, and salt and pepper to taste and cook, stirring, for 2 minutes. Cover and cook over low heat, stirring occasionally, for 10 minutes.

four Meanwhile, heat a little oil in a nonstick skillet. Add the tortilla wedges, in batches, and cook on both sides until crisp. Drain on paper towels. Transfer the wedges to a serving plate and top with the pork mixture, followed by the lettuce, a little sour cream, and some bell pepper. Garnish with a sprinkling of chili powder and serve at once with either some Pico de Gallo Salsa to add extra flavor or a batch of Taco Sauce to spoon over the pork.

To experience the classic hamburger you have to make it with the finest quality ground meat and serve it in a traditional sesame seed bap with plenty of caramelized onions and some ketchup.

prepare 10 minutes, plus 30 minutes' chilling
cook 16–25 minutes
serves 4–6

the classic hamburger

ingredients

1 lb/450 g freshly ground beef
1 onion, grated
2–4 garlic cloves, crushed
2 tsp whole grain mustard
pepper
2 tbsp olive oil
1 lb/450 g onions, finely sliced
2 tsp brown sugar

To serve

shredded iceberg lettuce
4–6 lightly toasted sesame seed baps
ketchup
French Fries

one Place the ground beef, onion, garlic, mustard, and pepper in a large bowl and mix together. Shape into 4–6 equal-size burgers, then cover and let chill for 30 minutes.

two Meanwhile, heat the oil in a heavy-bottom skillet. Add the onions and sauté over low heat for 8 minutes. Add the sugar and sauté for a further 5 minutes, until the onions have caramelized. Drain well on paper towels and keep warm.

three Wipe the skillet clean, then heat until hot. When hot, add the burgers and cook for 3–5 minutes on each side until cooked to personal preference. Arrange some shredded lettuce on the bases of the buns. Top with the burgers and then the onions. Spoon over a little ketchup and serve with French Fries.

These deliciously tender, thin pieces of breaded chicken, served in a classic sesame seed bun with ketchup or mayonnaise, go down wonderfully well with chicken and burger enthusiasts.

prepare 10 minutes, plus 30 minutes' chilling
cook 15–20 minutes
serves 4

the ultimate chicken burger

ingredients

4 chicken breast fillets, about 6 oz/175 g
    each, skinned
1 large egg white
1 tbsp cornstarch
1 tbsp all-purpose flour
1 egg, beaten
1 cup fresh white bread crumbs
2 tbsp corn oil

To serve
2 beefsteak tomatoes, sliced
shredded romaine lettuce
4 lightly toasted sesame seed buns
ketchup or mayonnaise
French Fries

one Place the chicken breasts between 2 sheets of nonstick parchment paper and flatten slightly using a meat mallet or a rolling pin. Beat the egg white and cornstarch together, then brush over the chicken. Cover and let chill for 30 minutes, then coat in the flour.

two Place the egg and bread crumbs in 2 separate bowls and coat the burgers first in the egg, allowing any excess to drip back into the bowl, then in the bread crumbs.

three Heat a heavy-bottom skillet and add the oil. When hot, add the burgers and cook over medium heat for 6–8 minutes on each side until thoroughly cooked. If you are in doubt, it is worth cutting one of the burgers in half. If there is any sign of pinkness, cook for a little longer. Add the tomato slices for the last 1–2 minutes of the cooking time to heat through.

four Place some lettuce on the bases of the buns. Top with the burgers, then the tomatoes. Spoon over a little ketchup and replace the lids. Serve with French Fries.

If you are feeling adventurous, try using a hotter variety of fresh chili in these burgers, such as a small Scotch Bonnet, habañero, or even Thai chili. Remember to seed them before using.

prepare 10 minutes,
plus 1 hour's chilling
cook 10–12 minutes
serves 4–6

three-bean burgers with green mayo

ingredients

10½ oz/300 g canned cannellini beans, drained

10½ oz/300 g canned black-eye peas, drained

10½ oz/300 g canned red kidney beans, drained and rinsed

1 fresh red chili, seeded

4 shallots, cut into quarters

2 celery stalks, coarsely chopped

1 cup fresh whole wheat bread crumbs

1 tbsp chopped fresh cilantro

2 tbsp whole wheat flour

2 tbsp corn oil

salt and pepper

Green mayo

6 tbsp prepared mayonnaise

2 tbsp chopped fresh parsley or mint

1 tbsp chopped cucumber

3 scallions, finely chopped

To serve

1 red and 1 yellow bell pepper, cored, seeded, and cut in half

few spinach leaves

4–6 lightly toasted sesame seed baps

Pico de Gallo Salsa

Spicy Potato Wedges

one Place the beans, chili, shallots, celery, bread crumbs, cilantro, and salt and pepper in a food processor and, using the pulse button, blend together. Shape into 4–6 equal-size burgers, then cover and let chill for 1 hour. Coat the burgers lightly in the flour.

two Heat a heavy-bottom skillet and add the oil. Also preheat the broiler. When the oil is hot, add the burgers and cook over medium heat for 5–6 minutes on each side until cooked and piping hot. Meanwhile, place the bell pepper halves, skin-side up, on an oiled broiler rack. Cook under the preheated hot broiler for 8–10 minutes until the flesh is soft and the skin is blackened and blistered. Leave to cool a little then cut into wedge shapes.

three Place the mayonnaise, parsley, cucumber, and scallions in a bowl and mix together. Place some spinach leaves on the bases of the buns with wedges of the charred bell pepper. Top with the burgers, then spoon over a little Green Mayo and some Pico de Gallo Salsa, and replace the lids on top. Serve with Spicy Potato Wedges.

Of all the cuts, tenderloin steak is the most expensive, but this is because it is the most tender, and it perfectly complements the shrimp in this recipe. This is a dish for entertaining in style!

prepare 20 minutes
cook 4–8 minutes
serves 2

surf 'n' turf skewers

ingredients

8 oz/225 g tenderloin steak, about
  1-inch/2.5-cm thick
8 raw unshelled jumbo shrimp
olive oil, for oiling
4 tbsp butter
2 garlic cloves, crushed

3 tbsp chopped fresh parsley, plus extra
  parsley sprigs, to garnish
finely grated rind and juice of 1 lime
salt and pepper
lime wedges, to garnish
crusty bread, to serve

one Cut the steak into 1-inch/2.5-cm cubes. To prepare the shrimp, use your fingers to pull off their heads then peel off their shells, leaving the tails on. Using a sharp knife, make a shallow slit along the underside of each shrimp, then pull out the dark vein and discard. Rinse the shrimp under cold running water and dry well on paper towels.

two Thread an equal number of the steak cubes and shrimp onto 4 oiled flat metal kabob skewers or presoaked wooden skewers. Season the kabobs to taste with pepper.

three Preheat the broiler to high. Meanwhile, put the butter and garlic into a small pan and heat gently until melted. Remove from the heat and add the parsley, lime rind and juice, and salt and pepper to taste. Leave in a warm place so that the butter remains melted.

four Brush the kabobs with a little of the melted butter. Put the kabobs onto an oiled broiler or grill rack and cook under or over medium heat for 4–8 minutes until the steak is cooked according to your taste and the shrimp turn pink, turning the kabobs frequently during cooking, and brushing with the remaining melted butter.

five Serve the kabobs hot on the skewers, with the remaining butter spooned over. Garnish with lime wedges and parsley sprigs and serve with crusty bread to mop up the buttery juices.

variations

Recipes for Surf 'n' Turf, otherwise known as "sea and shore," vary widely in America in different regions. Broiled or grilled steak and lobster is the most well-known pairing, but the surf can be crab, shrimp (as it is here), or scallops, and the turf can even be chicken.

Spice up your morning with these ranch-style or country-style eggs—an ideal dish for a weekend brunch. You can reduce the number of chilies if it's too early in the morning for a fiery hit.

prepare 15 minutes
cook 35–40 minutes
serves 4

huevos rancheros

ingredients

2 tbsp butter, bacon fat, or lard

2 onions, finely chopped

2 garlic cloves, finely chopped

2 red or yellow bell peppers, cored, seeded, and diced

2 fresh mild green chilies, seeded and finely chopped

4 large ripe tomatoes, peeled and chopped

2 tbsp lemon or lime juice

2 tsp dried oregano

4 large eggs

3 oz/75 g Cheddar cheese, grated

salt and pepper

To serve

warmed Flour Tortillas, or corn tortillas, or tortilla chips (optional)

toast or English muffins (optional)

one Preheat the oven to 350°F/180°C. Heat the butter in a heavy-bottom skillet over medium heat. Add the onions and garlic and cook, stirring frequently, for 5 minutes, or until softened. Add the bell peppers and chilies and cook for 5 minutes, or until softened.

two Add the tomatoes, lemon juice, and oregano and season to taste with salt and pepper. Bring to a boil, then reduce the heat, cover, and let simmer for 10 minutes, or until thickened, adding a little more lemon juice if the mixture becomes too dry.

three Transfer the mixture to a large ovenproof dish. Make 4 hollows in the mixture and break an egg into each. Bake in the oven for 12–15 minutes until the eggs are set.

four Sprinkle with grated cheese and return to the oven for 3–4 minutes until the cheese has melted. Serve immediately with traditional southwestern accompaniments, such as Flour Tortillas, corn tortillas or tortilla chips, or conventional breakfast fare, such as toast or English muffins, to mop up the delicious sauce.

Always popular for breakfast or brunch, French toast is the American version of the French *pain perdu*. The French title translates as "lost bread," referring to the day-old, slightly stale bread that is best to use for this sweet breakfast dish.

prepare 5 minutes

cook about 15 minutes, depending on the size of your pan

serves 4–6

french toast with maple syrup

ingredients

6 eggs
¾ cup milk
¼ tsp ground cinnamon
12 slices day-old challah or plain white bread

about 4 tbsp butter or margarine, plus extra to serve
½–1 tbsp sunflower-seed or corn oil
salt
warm maple syrup, to serve

one Preheat the oven to 275°F/140°C. Break the eggs into a large, shallow bowl and beat together with the milk, cinnamon, and salt to taste. Add the bread slices and press them down so that they are covered on both sides with the egg mixture. Leave the bread to stand for 1–2 minutes to soak up the egg mixture, turning the slices over once.

two Melt half the butter with ½ tablespoon of oil in a large skillet. Add as many bread slices as will fit in a single layer to the pan and cook for 2–3 minutes until golden brown.

three Turn the bread slices over and cook until golden brown on the other side. Transfer the French toast to a plate and keep warm in the oven while cooking the remaining bread slices, adding extra oil if necessary.

four Serve the French toast with the remaining butter melting on top and warm maple syrup for pouring over.

did you know?

One sure hint that spring is on its way is when maple syrup tapping begins in Ohio, Illinois, Indiana, Michigan, Minnesota, and Pennsylvania. Today's production procedure doesn't differ much from when European settlers were taught the technique by Native Americans. The sap is caught in buckets when the maple trees are tapped and then boiled in sugarhouses until the golden syrup forms—a process called "sugaring."

These spicy muffins are quick and easy to make with a few stock ingredients and two small apples. The crunchy sugar topping turns them into a truly fruity treat.

prepare 15 minutes
cook 20–25 minutes
makes 6

apple and cinnamon muffins

ingredients

⅔ cup whole wheat all-purpose flour
½ cup white all-purpose flour
1½ tsp baking powder
pinch of salt
1 tsp ground cinnamon
scant ¼ cup golden superfine sugar
2 small eating apples, peeled, cored,
    and finely chopped
½ cup milk
1 egg, beaten
4 tbsp butter, melted

Topping
12 brown sugar lumps, coarsely crushed
½ tsp ground cinnamon

one Preheat the oven to 400°F/200°C. Line 6 holes of a muffin pan with paper muffin cases.

two Sift the 2 flours, baking powder, salt, and cinnamon into a large bowl and stir in the sugar and chopped apples. Place the milk, egg, and butter in a separate bowl and mix. Add the wet ingredients to the dry ingredients and gently stir until just combined.

three Divide the mixture between the paper cases. To make the topping, mix together the crushed sugar lumps and cinnamon and sprinkle over the muffins. Bake in the preheated oven for 20–25 minutes until risen and golden. Serve warm or cold.

cook's tip

Work quickly once you have chopped the apple, as the flesh soon starts to brown on exposure to the air.

variation

If you like, you can split this mixture into 12 portions to make small muffins.

When it's summer in Maine, the state's blueberries feature at every meal, starting with breakfast, when they flavor muffins and pancakes. For a complete New England breakfast, serve these with Vermont maple syrup.

prepare 10 minutes
cook 15–20 minutes
makes 10–12 pancakes

blueberry pancakes

ingredients

1 cup all-purpose flour
2 tbsp superfine sugar
2 tsp baking powder
½ tsp salt
1 cup buttermilk
3 tbsp butter, melted
1 large egg
5 oz/140 g blueberries, rinsed and
    patted dry
sunflower-seed or corn oil, for greasing

To serve
butter
warm maple syrup

cook's tip

Cook blueberry pancakes over a slightly lower heat than other pancakes, otherwise the high concentration of sugar in the berries can cause them to burn.

one Preheat the oven to 275°F/140°C. Sift the flour, sugar, baking powder, and salt together into a large bowl and make a well in the center.

two Beat the buttermilk, butter, and egg together in a separate small bowl, then pour the mixture into the well in the dry ingredients. Beat the dry ingredients into the liquid, gradually drawing them in from the side, until a smooth batter forms. Gently stir in the blueberries.

three Heat a large skillet over medium-high heat until a splash of water dances on the surface. Use a pastry brush or crumpled piece of paper towel and the oil to lightly grease the base of the skillet.

four Use a ladle to drop about 4 tablespoons of batter into the skillet and spread it out into a 4-inch/10-cm round. Continue adding as many pancakes as will fit in your skillet. Leave the pancakes to cook until small bubbles appear on the surface, then flip them over and cook for a further 1–2 minutes until the bottoms are golden brown.

five Transfer the pancakes to a warmed plate and keep warm in the oven while you cook the remaining batter, lightly greasing the skillet as before. Serve with a pat of butter on top of each pancake and warm maple syrup for pouring over.

main courses

It wouldn't be Fourth of July in the South without a barbecue. For many, the phrase "come to a barbecue" means cooking a whole hog in a pit, but this recipe is more suited to a home "cookout."

prepare 15 minutes,
plus 8 hours' marinating
cook 1½–2 hours
serves 4–6

barbecue rack of ribs

ingredients

2 racks of pork ribs, about 1 lb 7 oz/650 g
   each
vegetable oil, for brushing

Tennessee rub

1 tbsp ground cumin
1 tsp garlic salt
½ tsp ground cinnamon
½ tsp dry English mustard powder
½ tsp ground coriander
1 tsp dried mixed herbs
pinch of cayenne pepper, or to taste

Bourbon barbecue sauce

1 tbsp corn or peanut oil
½ onion, finely chopped
2 large garlic cloves, minced
generous ⅓ cup brown sugar
1 tbsp dry English mustard powder
1 tsp ground cumin
2 tbsp tomato paste
6 tbsp bourbon
2 tbsp Worcestershire sauce
2 tbsp apple or white wine vinegar
few drops of hot pepper sauce, to taste

one A day ahead, mix all the ingredients for the rub together in a small bowl. Rub the mixture onto both sides of the ribs, then cover and let marinate in the refrigerator overnight.

two To make the Barbecue Sauce, heat the oil in a pan over medium-high heat. Add the onion and garlic and cook for 5 minutes, stirring frequently, or until the onion is soft. Stir in the remaining sauce ingredients. Slowly bring to a boil, stirring to dissolve the sugar, then reduce the heat and let simmer, uncovered, for 30 minutes–1 hour, stirring occasionally, until dark brown and very thick. Let cool, then cover and let chill until required.

three When ready to barbecue, heat the coals until they are glowing. Brush the barbecue rack with a little oil. Put the ribs onto the rack and cook, turning frequently, for 40 minutes, or until the meat feels tender. If they appear to be drying out, brush with water.

four Remove the ribs from the barbecue and, when cool enough to handle, cut them into 1- or 2-rib portions. Return the rib portions to the barbecue and baste with the sauce. Cook the ribs, turning frequently and basting generously with the sauce, for an additional 10 minutes, or until they are dark brown and glossy. Serve with any remaining sauce, reheated, to use for dipping—and plenty of paper napkins for sticky fingers!

This is undoubtedly the steak recipe that you will turn to time and time again, and even if you don't have a broiler, all is not lost. Using a thick, cast-iron stove-top grill pan or griddle instead, preheat it and cook the steaks as in the recipe.

prepare 5 minutes,
plus 2 hours' chilling
cook 5–20 minutes
serves 6

the perfect broiled steak

ingredients

6 rump, sirloin, or tenderloin steaks,
   about 6–8 oz/175–225 g each
olive or sunflower-seed oil, for brushing
   and oiling
pepper

Maître d'hôtel butter
½ cup butter
3 tbsp finely chopped fresh parsley
1 tbsp lemon juice
salt and pepper

To serve
jacket baked potatoes
green salad

one To make the Maître d'Hôtel Butter, put the butter into a bowl and beat with a wooden spoon until softened. Add the parsley and lemon juice, season to taste with salt and pepper, and blend together until well mixed. Turn the mixture out onto a sheet of waxed paper and shape into a roll. Wrap in the waxed paper and let chill in the refrigerator for 2–3 hours until firm. Just before serving, slice into thin circles. Preheat the broiler or barbecue. Brush each steak with oil and season to taste with pepper.

two Put each steak onto an oiled broiler or grill rack and cook under or over medium heat for the required length of time and according to your taste: for ¾-inch/2-cm thick steaks, 5 minutes for rare, 8–10 minutes for medium, and 12–14 minutes for well done; for 1-inch/2.5-cm thick steaks, 6–7 minutes for rare, 8–10 minutes for medium, and 12–15 minutes for well done; for 1½-inch/4-cm thick steaks, 10 minutes for rare, 12–14 minutes for medium, and 18–20 minutes for well done. During cooking, turn the steaks frequently, using a spatula rather than a sharp tool so that you don't pierce the meat and allow the juices to escape. When you turn the steaks, brush them once or twice with oil. Watch the steaks constantly during cooking to ensure that they don't overcook.

three Serve immediately, each perfectly broiled steak topped with a slice of Maître d'Hôtel Butter and accompanied by a jacket baked potato and green salad.

cook's tip

If the steaks have a piece of fat running along them, cut or snip into it at regular intervals to prevent the steaks from curling during cooking. A jacket baked potato has been suggested as a healthy accompaniment to the steaks, but you could serve them with French Fries and Crispy Onion Rings instead.

This dish still takes its name from the 19th-century physician Dr. James H. Salisbury, who would prescribe beef patties as remedies for a whole range of different ailments.

prepare 5 minutes
cook 15 minutes
serves 4

salisbury steak

ingredients

4 tbsp vegetable oil

2–3 large onions, thinly sliced

16 white mushrooms, thinly sliced

2 cups freshly ground beef

1 ciabatta loaf

4 tomatoes, sliced (optional)

1 cup red wine or beef stock

salt and pepper

one Heat the oil in a skillet over high heat. Add the onion and mushrooms and cook quickly until soft. Push the vegetables to the side of the skillet.

two Season the beef to taste with salt and pepper, then shape into four round patties. Add to the skillet and cook, in batches if necessary, until starting to brown, then carefully flip over and cook the other sides. Slice the ciabatta horizontally through the center and cut into quarters, then toast lightly and arrange on a serving dish. Top with the tomato slices, if using.

three Remove the meat patties from the skillet and set them on the ciabatta slices.

four Bring the onions and mushrooms back to the center of the skillet, pour over the wine, and heat until boiling. Continue boiling for 1 minute, or until slightly reduced, then remove from the heat and spoon over the meat patties. Serve immediately.

This is a decadent dish for lovers of bleu cheese. Serve it when entertaining, or use individual sirloin or rump steaks as an alternative to the whole tenderloin when serving as a family meal.

prepare 20 minutes
cook 20–30 minutes
serves 6

tenderloin steak with bleu cheese sauce

ingredients

1 tenderloin steak, about 3 lb/1.3 kg

5 tbsp butter

olive or vegetable oil, for oiling

4½ oz/125 g bleu cheese, crumbled (see Cook's Tip)

1 shallot, minced

generous ⅓ cup Madeira or dry sherry

⅔ cup heavy cream

salt and pepper

chopped fresh parsley, to garnish

freshly cooked green beans, to serve

cook's tip

You need a semihard bleu cheese for this recipe. Choose from Italian Gorgonzola, French Roquefort, English Stilton, or Danish Blue, depending upon availability and your personal choice.

one Preheat the broiler or barbecue. Tie the tenderloin widthwise at regular intervals with string to form a neat shape. Put the butter into a small bowl and beat with a wooden spoon until softened. Spread 2 tablespoons of the softened butter evenly all over the tenderloin. Season to taste with pepper.

two Put the tenderloin onto an oiled broiler or grill rack and cook under or over high heat, turning frequently, until browned on all sides, then cook at medium heat for 18–25 minutes, according to your taste, turning frequently.

three Meanwhile, add the bleu cheese to the remaining softened butter and blend together until the mixture is smooth.

four Put the shallot and Madeira into a pan, bring to a boil, and boil until reduced to about 2 tablespoons. Stir in the cream, then let simmer for 3 minutes. Add the cheese mixture, a little at a time, whisking after each addition until the sauce is smooth. When all the cheese mixture has been added, remove from the heat. Season to taste with salt and pepper.

five Transfer the cooked tenderloin to a warmed serving dish and let rest for 5 minutes. Slice the tenderloin into steaks and serve with green beans and the bleu cheese sauce drizzled over, garnished with chopped parsley. Serve any remaining sauce separately in a pitcher.

This is an adaptation of the classic steak au poivre, which is served with a sauce containing cream. If wished, you could add about ⅔ cup of heavy cream to the reduced pan juices at the final stage to mellow the fiery heat of the peppercorns.

prepare 15 minutes
cook 7–16 minutes
serves 2

peppered t-bone steaks

ingredients

2 tbsp whole black peppercorns, green
   peppercorns, or a mixture of both
2 T-bone steaks, about 9 oz/250 g each
2 tbsp butter
1 tbsp olive or sunflower-seed oil
½ cup red wine
salt

To serve

freshly cooked green beans
long-grain rice, cooked with turmeric for
   added color

one Put the peppercorns into a mortar and coarsely crush with a pestle, or put into a strong plastic bag, place on a cutting board, and coarsely crush with the end of a rolling pin.

two Spread the crushed peppercorns out on a plate and press one side of each steak hard into them to encrust the surface of the meat. Turn over and repeat with the other side.

three Melt the butter with the oil in a large, heavy-bottom skillet over high heat. When hot, add the steaks and cook quickly on both sides to seal. Reduce the heat to medium and cook, turning once, for 2½–3 minutes each side for rare, 3½–5 minutes each side for medium, or 5–7 minutes each side for well done. Transfer the steaks to warmed plates and keep warm.

four Add the wine to the skillet and stir to deglaze by scraping any sediment from the bottom of the skillet. Bring to a boil and boil until reduced by about half. Season to taste with salt. Pour the pan juices over the steaks and serve immediately with freshly cooked beans and rice.

did you know?

It is mainly Texas that supplies America with huge T-bone steaks. On one side of the bone is the sirloin, with its strip of fat running along the edge, and on the other side is the fillet. It is a juicy cut with a good flavor that is suitable for pan-frying, broiling, or grilling —and will satisfy anyone with a large appetite!

This is a typical southwestern-style chili, with chunks of beef rather than ground meat and without beans. Purists would also omit onions. Chocolate—a taste of old Mexico—gives extra depth to the sauce.

prepare 15 minutes
cook 2½–3½ hours
serves 4

lone star chili

ingredients

1 tbsp cumin seeds

1 lb 7 oz/650 g rump steak, cut into 1-inch/2.5-cm cubes

all-purpose flour, well seasoned with salt and pepper, for coating

3 tbsp beef drippings, bacon fat, or vegetable oil

2 onions, finely chopped

4 garlic cloves, finely chopped

1 tbsp dried oregano

2 tsp paprika

4 dried red chilies, such as ancho or pasilla, crushed, or to taste

1 large bottle of South American lager

4 squares semisweet chocolate

To serve

warmed Flour Tortillas

sour cream

one Dry-fry the cumin seeds in a heavy-bottom skillet over medium heat, shaking the skillet, for 3–4 minutes until lightly toasted. Let cool, then crush in a mortar with a pestle. Alternatively, use a coffee grinder.

two Toss the beef in the seasoned flour to coat. Melt the fat in a large, heavy-bottom pan. Add the beef, in batches, and cook until browned on all sides. Remove the beef with a slotted spoon and set aside.

three Add the onions and garlic to the pan and cook gently for 5 minutes, or until softened. Add the cumin, oregano, paprika, and chilies and cook, stirring, for 2 minutes. Return the beef to the pan, pour over the lager, then add the chocolate. Bring to a boil, stirring, then reduce the heat, cover, and let simmer for 2–3 hours until the beef is very tender, adding more lager if necessary.

four Serve with warmed Flour Tortillas and some sour cream to douse the flames. Wash it down with some additional ice-cold beer of your choice.

This is a dish for those seriously committed to comfort eating. It would be equally effective with good-quality ground beef, if you prefer.

prepare 15 minutes
cook 45 minutes
serves 4

beef enchiladas

ingredients

2 tbsp olive oil, plus extra for oiling

2 large onions, thinly sliced

1 lb 4 oz/550 g lean beef, cut into bite-size pieces

1 tbsp ground cumin

1–2 tsp cayenne pepper, or to taste

1 tsp paprika

8 soft corn tortillas

8 oz/225 g Cheddar cheese, grated

salt and pepper

Taco sauce

1 tbsp olive oil

1 onion, finely chopped

1 green bell pepper, seeded and diced

1–2 fresh hot green chilies, such as

jalapeño, seeded and finely chopped

3 garlic cloves, crushed

1 tsp ground cumin

1 tsp ground coriander

1 tsp brown sugar

1 lb/450 g ripe tomatoes, peeled and coarsely chopped

juice of ½ lemon

To serve

shredded iceberg lettuce

1 red onion, finely chopped

1 avocado, peeled, stoned, and cubed

lime juice

Pico de Gallo Salsa

Refried Beans

one Preheat the oven to 350°F/180°C. Oil a large, rectangular baking dish. To make the Taco Sauce, heat the oil in a deep skillet over medium heat. Add the onion and cook for 5 minutes, or until softened. Add the bell pepper and chilies and cook for 5 minutes. Add the garlic, cumin, coriander, and sugar and cook the sauce for an additional 2 minutes, stirring. Add the tomatoes, lemon juice, and salt and pepper to taste. Bring to a boil, then reduce the heat and let simmer for 10 minutes. Remove from the heat and set aside.

two Heat the oil in a large skillet over low heat. Add the onions and cook for 10 minutes, or until soft. Remove with a slotted spoon and set aside. Increase the heat to high, add the beef, and cook, stirring, for 2–3 minutes until browned all over. Reduce the heat to medium, add the spices and salt and pepper to taste, and cook, stirring constantly, for 2 minutes.

three Warm each tortilla in a lightly oiled nonstick skillet for 15 seconds on each side, then dip each in the Taco Sauce. Top each with beef, onions, and cheese and roll up. Place seam-side down in the prepared baking dish, top with the remaining sauce and grated cheese, and bake in the oven for 30 minutes. Serve at once with lettuce, onion, avocado dipped in lime juice to prevent discoloration, Pico de Gallo Salsa, and Refried Beans.

This dish was brought over by early German settlers. Long marinating makes the topside melt-in-the-mouth tender and imparts a marvelous spicy flavor. This is the perfect treat for a special occasion.

prepare 20 minutes,
plus 48 hours' marinating
cook 2¼ hours
serves 4

sauerbraten

ingredients

1 lb 10 oz/750 g top round of beef,
   trimmed of all visible fat
8 whole cloves
1 tbsp corn oil
1 cup good-quality beef stock
2 lb 4 oz/1 kg mixed root vegetables, such
   as carrots, potatoes, and rutabaga,
   peeled and cut into chunks
2 tbsp raisins
1½ tsp cornstarch
3 tbsp water
salt and pepper

Marinade
¾ cup wine
5 tbsp red wine vinegar
1 onion, chopped
1½ tsp brown sugar
4 peppercorns
1 bay leaf
½ tsp ground allspice
½ tsp mustard

variation

Try other root vegetables with this dish, such as chunks of parsnip, turnip, and celery root.

one To make the marinade, put all the ingredients, except the mustard, in a pan. Bring to simmering point, then remove from the heat and stir in the mustard. Stud the beef with cloves and place in a nonmetallic dish. Pour the marinade over, cover, and let cool, then let chill in the refrigerator for 2 days. About 1 hour before cooking, remove the beef, pat dry, and let stand at room temperature. Set aside the marinade.

two Preheat the oven to 300°F/150°C. Heat the oil in an ovenproof casserole, add the beef, and cook over medium heat for 5–10 minutes until browned. Pour the marinade into the casserole through a strainer, add the stock, and bring to a boil. Cover and bake in the oven for 1 hour, turning and basting frequently with the cooking juices.

three Meanwhile, blanch the vegetables in boiling water for 3 minutes, then drain. Arrange the vegetables around the beef, return to the oven, and cook for 1 hour, or until the beef is very tender and the vegetables are cooked.

four Transfer the beef and vegetables to a warmed serving dish. Place the casserole on low heat and add the raisins. Mix the cornstarch and water until smooth and stir into the cooking juices. Bring to a boil, stirring, then let simmer for 2–3 minutes. Season and serve.

There are almost as many meatloaf recipes in the world as there are cooks—this version is a very traditional recipe, using basic ingredients to create a hearty meatloaf that everyone will remember fondly.

meatloaf

ingredients

1 thick slice crustless white bread
3 cups freshly ground beef, pork, or lamb
1 small egg
1 tbsp finely chopped onion
1 beef bouillon cube, crumbled
1 tsp dried herbs
salt and pepper

To serve
tomato or mushroom sauce or gravy
mashed potatoes
freshly cooked green beans

one Preheat the oven to 350°F/180°C.

two Put the bread into a small bowl and add enough water to soak. Let stand for 5 minutes, then drain and squeeze well to get rid of all the water.

three Combine the bread and all the other ingredients in a bowl. Shape into a loaf, then place on a cookie sheet or in an ovenproof dish. Put the meatloaf in the oven and cook for 30–45 minutes until the juices run clear when it is pierced with a toothpick.

four Serve in slices with your favorite sauce or gravy, mashed potatoes, and green beans.

In this dish which is popular with both children and adults, delicious, bite-size meatballs are simmered in a rich tomato sauce and served on a bed of freshly cooked spaghetti.

prepare 20 minutes, plus 30 minutes' chilling
cook 45 minutes
serves 6

spaghetti and meatballs

ingredients

1 oz/25 g white bread, crusts removed and torn into pieces
2 tbsp milk
2 cups freshly ground beef
4 tbsp chopped fresh flat-leaf parsley
1 egg
pinch of cayenne pepper
2 tbsp olive oil
²/₃ cup strained canned tomatoes
7 oz/200 g canned chopped tomatoes
1¾ cups vegetable stock
pinch of sugar
1 lb/450 g dried spaghetti
salt and pepper

cook's tip

When forming the meat mixture into balls, dampen your hands slightly with a little cold water to help prevent the mixture sticking.

variation

For a spicier version, substitute a pinch of crushed, dried red chili for the cayenne and stir ½ teaspoon crushed chili into the sauce with the sugar.

one Place the bread in a small bowl, add the milk, and let soak. Meanwhile, place the beef in a large bowl and add half the parsley, the egg, and the cayenne pepper. Season to taste with salt and pepper. Squeeze the excess moisture out of the bread and crumble it over the meat mixture. Mix well until smooth.

two Form small pieces of the mixture into balls between the palms of your hands and place on a baking sheet or board. Let chill in the refrigerator for 30 minutes.

three Heat the olive oil in a heavy-bottom skillet. Add the meatballs in batches, and cook, stirring and turning frequently, until browned on all sides. Return earlier batches to the skillet, add the strained tomatoes, chopped tomatoes and their can juices, vegetable stock, and sugar, then season to taste with salt and pepper. Bring to a boil, reduce the heat, cover, and let simmer for 25–30 minutes until the sauce is thickened and the meatballs are tender and cooked through.

four Meanwhile, bring a large pan of lightly salted water to a boil. Add the pasta, return to a boil, and cook for 8–10 minutes until tender but still firm to the bite. Drain and transfer to a warmed serving dish. Pour the sauce over the pasta and toss lightly. Sprinkle with the remaining parsley and serve immediately.

From Wisconsin, this is a good recipe to have up your sleeve when there is a gang to feed. Simmering the bratwurst sausages in lager keeps them tender and moist.

prepare 15 minutes
cook about 45 minutes, depending on the size of your pan
serves 4

sausages and onions

ingredients

8 fresh bratwurst sausages, pricked all over with a fork

about 2 tbsp sunflower-seed or corn oil (as required)

2 onions, thinly sliced

2 garlic cloves, sliced

2 cups pilsner lager

1 tbsp German brown mustard or coarse-grain mustard, plus extra to serve

salt and pepper

chunks of Italian or French bread, to serve

one Heat a large skillet or flameproof casserole with a tight-fitting lid over medium-high heat. Add as many sausages as will fit in a single layer and cook, stirring frequently, until brown all over. Remove from the skillet and set aside. Brown the remaining sausages, if necessary.

two Add extra oil to the sausage fat in the skillet, if necessary, to make about 2 tablespoons in total. Add the onions to the pan and cook, stirring frequently, for 5 minutes. Add the garlic and cook, stirring frequently, for a further 5 minutes, or until the onions are soft and lightly browned.

three Stir in the beer, scraping the base of the skillet with a wooden spoon. Return the sausages to the skillet. Increase the heat to high and bring the beer to the boil, then reduce the heat to low, cover tightly and simmer for 20 minutes.

four Stir in the mustard and simmer, uncovered, for a few minutes until most of the lager has evaporated. Season to taste with salt and pepper.

five Serve the sausages split lengthwise down the center with the onions spooned over. Serve with chunks of bread and a small jar of mustard on the side.

variations

For a meal on the run, divide the sausages and onions between toasted hot dog buns. Or try sliced cooked "brats" on a hard Kaiser or other hard roll with a selection of onions and pickles for another Minnesota favorite.

It's a southern tradition to invite friends and family in for a bowl of Hoppin' John on New Year's Day. Legend maintains that the more black-eye peas you eat, the more prosperous the year will be. Whereas, without a bowl of Hoppin' John, only bad luck will follow.

prepare 10 minutes, plus 8 hours' soaking

cook 3½–4 hours

serves 4

hoppin' john

ingredients

1 unsmoked ham hock, weighing 2 lb 12 oz/1.25 kg

1 cup dried black-eye peas, soaked overnight

2 large celery stalks, broken in half

1 bay leaf

1 large onion, chopped

1 dried red chili (optional)

1 tbsp rendered bacon fat, or corn or peanut oil

1 cup Carolina long-grain rice

salt and pepper

To serve

hot pepper sauce

freshly cooked greens

one Put the ham hock into a large, flameproof casserole with water to cover over high heat. Bring to a boil, skimming the surface. Cover, reduce the heat, and let simmer for 1½ hours.

two Stir in the drained peas, celery, bay leaf, onion, and chili, if using, and let simmer for an additional 1½–2 hours, or until the peas are tender but not mushy and the ham hock feels tender when you prod it with a knife.

three Strain the "pot likker" (as the cooking liquid is described in old recipes) into a large bowl and reserve. Set the ham hock aside and set the peas aside separately, removing and discarding the flavorings.

four Heat the bacon fat in a pan or flameproof casserole with a tight-fitting lid over medium heat. Add the rice and stir until coated with the fat. Stir in 2 cups of the reserved cooking liquid, the peas, and salt and pepper to taste. (Use the remaining cooking liquid for soup, or discard.) Bring to a boil, stirring constantly, then reduce the heat to very low, cover, and let simmer for 20 minutes without lifting the lid.

five Meanwhile, cut the meat from the ham hock, discarding the skin and excess fat. Cut the meat into bite-size pieces.

six Remove the pan from the heat and let stand for 5 minutes, again without lifting the lid. Fluff up the rice and peas with a fork and stir in the ham, then pile onto a warmed serving dish. Serve with a bottle of hot pepper sauce on the side and some cooked greens and cornbread.

This is a stew of southern climes rather than the chilly north, full of warm, sunny flavors. Mexican oregano is rather different from the Mediterranean variety, but the latter still works well here.

prepare 25 minutes
cook 2 hours
serves 4–6

spicy pork and vegetable hotchpotch

ingredients

1 lb/450 g lean boneless pork, cut into
    1-inch/2.5-cm cubes

all-purpose flour, well seasoned with salt
    and pepper, for coating

1 tbsp vegetable oil

8 oz/225 g chorizo sausage, outer casing
    removed, cut into bite-size chunks

1 onion, coarsely chopped

4 garlic cloves, finely chopped

2 celery stalks, chopped

1 cinnamon stick, broken

2 bay leaves

2 tsp allspice

2 carrots, sliced

2–3 fresh red chilies, seeded and
    finely chopped

6 ripe tomatoes, peeled and chopped

4 cups pork or vegetable stock

2 sweet potatoes, cut into chunks

corn kernels, cut from 1 ear fresh corn

1 tbsp chopped fresh oregano, plus extra
    oregano sprigs to garnish

salt and pepper

cooked long-grain rice, to serve

one Toss the pork in the seasoned flour to coat. Heat the oil in a large, heavy-bottom pan or ovenproof casserole. Add the chorizo and lightly brown on all sides. Remove the chorizo with a slotted spoon and set aside.

two Add the pork, in batches, and cook until browned on all sides. Remove the pork with a slotted spoon and set aside. Add the onion, garlic, and celery to the pan and cook for 5 minutes, or until softened.

three Add the cinnamon, bay leaves, and allspice and cook, stirring, for 2 minutes. Add the pork, carrots, chilies, tomatoes, and stock. Bring to a boil, then reduce the heat, cover, and let simmer for 1 hour, or until the pork is tender.

four Return the chorizo to the pan with the sweet potatoes, corn, oregano, and salt and pepper to taste. Cover and let simmer for an additional 30 minutes, or until the vegetables are tender. Discard the bay leaves. Serve garnished with oregano sprigs, and with some plain boiled long-grain rice to absorb some of the sauce.

Lamb shanks come into their own when slowly simmered in red wine, flavored with vegetables and orange, and need little attention as they do so. It is a dish that was brought to America by Italian emigrants.

prepare 25 minutes
cook 2½ hours
serves 4

braised lamb shanks with cannellini beans

ingredients

9 oz/250 g cannellini beans, soaked
   overnight
2 tbsp sunflower-seed or corn oil
1 large onion, thinly sliced
4 carrots, chopped
2 celery sticks, thinly sliced
1 garlic clove, chopped
4 large lamb shanks

14 oz/400 g canned chopped tomatoes
1¼ cups red wine
finely pared zest and juice of 1 orange
2 bay leaves
3 rosemary sprigs
scant 1 cup water
salt and pepper
chopped fresh parsley, to garnish

cook's tip

If you don't have time to soak the cannellini beans overnight, or have simply forgotten, all is not lost. Put them in a pan of water, bring to a boil, simmer for 2 minutes, and then leave to soak for 2–3 hours before using. As a last resort, you could add two 14½ oz/410 g cans drained cannellini beans 30 minutes before the end of cooking, but the flavor will not be as superior as the beans will not have had the chance to absorb the flavors of the stew.

one Preheat the oven to 325°F/160°C. Drain the soaked beans and rinse under cold running water. Put in a large pan of cold water, bring to a boil, and skim off any scum, then boil rapidly for 10 minutes. Drain and set aside when boiled.

two Meanwhile, heat the oil in a large, flameproof casserole, add the onion, and fry for 5 minutes, or until softened. Add the carrots and celery and fry for a further 5 minutes, or until beginning to soften and the onion is beginning to brown. Add the garlic and fry for a further 1 minute. Push the vegetables to the sides of the pan.

three Add the lamb shanks to the pan and fry for about 5 minutes, until browned on all sides. Add the beans to the pan with the tomatoes, wine, and orange zest and juice and stir together. Add the bay leaves and rosemary. Pour in the water so that the liquid comes halfway up the shanks. Season with pepper but do not add salt as this will stop the beans softening.

four Bring to a boil, then cover the pan and cook in the oven for about 1 hour. Turn the shanks over in the stock then continue cooking for 1½ hours until the lamb and beans are tender. Remove the bay leaves, then taste and add salt and pepper if necessary. Serve hot, garnished with chopped parsley.

This is the signature dish of the South. Everywhere south of the Mason-Dixon line, fried chicken—golden and crisp on the outside, with tender flesh on the inside—is on the menu.

prepare 10 minutes, plus 4 hours' soaking
cook 20–40 minutes, depending on the size of your pan
serves 4–6

southern fried chicken

ingredients

1 chicken, weighing 3 lb 5 oz/1.5 kg, cut into 6 or 8 pieces

½ cup all-purpose flour

2–4 tbsp butter

corn or peanut oil, for pan-frying

salt and pepper

To serve

mashed potato

A Pot of Southern Peas

one Put the chicken into a large bowl with 1 teaspoon of salt and cold water to cover, then cover the bowl and let stand in the refrigerator for at least 4 hours, but ideally overnight. Drain the chicken pieces well and pat completely dry with paper towels.

two Put the flour and salt and pepper to taste into a plastic bag, hold closed, and shake to mix. Add the chicken pieces and shake until well coated. Remove the chicken pieces from the bag and shake off any excess flour.

three Melt 2 tablespoons of the butter with about ½ inch/1 cm of oil in an ovenproof casserole or large skillet with a lid over medium-high heat.

four Add as many chicken pieces as will fit in a single layer without overcrowding, skin-side down. Cook for 5 minutes, or until the skin is golden and crisp. Turn the chicken over and cook for an additional 10–15 minutes, covered, until it is tender and the juices run clear when a skewer is inserted into the thickest part of the meat. Remove the chicken from the casserole with a slotted spoon and drain well on paper towels. Transfer to a low oven to keep warm while cooking any remaining pieces, if necessary, or let cool completely. Remove any brown bits from the dish and melt the remaining butter in the oil, adding more oil as needed, to cook the next batch. Serve hot or cold with mashed potato and a Pot of Southern Peas.

variations

Southerners have strong opinions about how to fry chicken, and there are as many "authentic" recipes as there are southern cooks: buttermilk can replace water for soaking; cayenne pepper, paprika, and dried thyme season the flour; cornmeal replaces the flour; bacon fat, lard, or butter are used for cooking.

This Cajun dish is borrowed from Spain, where it originated. Its lively mixture of chicken and shrimp makes it a good dish to serve at a brunch party, instead of the more traditional kedgeree.

prepare 20 minutes
cook 50–55 minutes
serves 6

jambalaya

ingredients

2 tbsp lard

3 lb 5 oz/1.5 kg chicken pieces

2½ tbsp all-purpose flour

8 oz/225 g rindless smoked gammon, diced

1 onion, chopped

1 orange bell pepper, cored, seeded, and sliced

12 oz/350 g tomatoes, peeled and chopped

1 garlic clove, finely chopped

1 tsp chopped fresh thyme

12 raw, shelled jumbo shrimp

generous 1 cup long-grain rice

scant 2 cups chicken stock or water

dash of Tabasco sauce

3 scallions, finely chopped

2 tbsp chopped fresh flat-leaf parsley, plus extra sprigs, to garnish

salt and pepper

cook's tip

If you like an even hotter taste, add 1 teaspoon of cayenne pepper with the seasoning in Step 3.

variation

If you don't want to use lard in this recipe, substitute 2 tablespoons of corn oil.

one Melt the lard in a large, flameproof casserole. Add the chicken and cook over medium heat, turning occasionally, for 8–10 minutes until golden brown all over. Transfer the chicken to a plate using tongs.

two Add the flour to the casserole and cook over very low heat, stirring, for 15 minutes, or until golden brown. Do not let it burn. Return the chicken pieces to the casserole with the gammon, onion, bell pepper, tomatoes, garlic, and thyme. Cook, stirring frequently, for 10 minutes.

three Stir in the shrimp, rice, and stock, and season to taste with Tabasco and salt and pepper. Bring the mixture to a boil, reduce the heat, cover, and cook for 15–20 minutes until all of the liquid has been absorbed and the rice is tender. Stir in the scallions and chopped parsley, garnish with parsley sprigs, and serve.

A cross between a soup and a stew, gumbo is one of the great dishes
of Louisiana Creole cooking. All gumbos begin with the essential slowly
cooked roux, and are then thickened with okra or filé.

prepare 20 minutes
cook 2¼ hours
serves 4–6

chicken gumbo

ingredients

1 chicken, weighing 3 lb 5 oz/1.5 kg,
  cut into 6 pieces
2 celery stalks, 1 broken in half and
  1 finely chopped
1 carrot, chopped
2 onions, 1 sliced and 1 chopped
2 bay leaves
4 tbsp corn or peanut oil
½ cup all-purpose flour
2 large garlic cloves, crushed

1 green bell pepper, cored, seeded,
  and diced
1 lb/450 g fresh okra, trimmed, then cut
  crosswise into ½-inch/1-cm slices
8 oz/225 g andouille sausage or Polish
  kielbasa, sliced
2 tbsp tomato paste
1 tsp dried thyme
½ tsp salt
½ tsp cayenne pepper

¼ tsp pepper
14 oz/400 g canned peeled
  plum tomatoes
salt

To serve
cooked long-grain rice
hot pepper sauce

one Put the chicken into a large pan with water to cover over medium-high heat and bring to
a boil, skimming the surface to remove the foam. When the foam stops rising, reduce the heat
to medium, add the celery stalk halves, carrot, sliced onion, 1 bay leaf, and ¼ teaspoon of
salt and let simmer for 20 minutes, or until the chicken is tender and the juices run clear
when a skewer is inserted into the thickest part of the meat. Strain the chicken, reserving
4 cups of the liquid. When the chicken is cool enough to handle, remove and discard all the
skin, bones, and flavorings. Cut the flesh into bite-size pieces and set aside.

two Heat the oil in a large pan over medium-high heat for 2 minutes. Reduce the heat to low,
sprinkle in the flour, and stir to make the roux. Stir constantly for 30 minutes, or until the roux
turns hazelnut-brown. If black specks appear, it is burned and you will have to start again.

three Add the chopped celery, chopped onion, garlic, bell pepper, and okra to the pan.
Increase the heat to medium-high and cook, stirring frequently, for 5 minutes. Add the
sausage and cook, stirring frequently, for 2 minutes.

four Stir in the remaining ingredients, including the second bay leaf, and the reserved
cooking liquid. Bring to a boil, crushing the tomatoes with a wooden spoon. Reduce the heat
to medium-low and let simmer, uncovered, for 30 minutes, stirring occasionally.

five Add the chicken to the pan and let simmer for an additional 30 minutes. Taste and
adjust the seasoning, if necessary. Discard the bay leaf and spoon the gumbo over the rice
and serve with a bottle of hot pepper sauce on the side.

This recipe features a famed sauce, Mole Poblano, renowned for its surprising pairing of chocolate and chili. The result is sumptuous rather than strange, with a deep, rich, mellow quality.

prepare 20 minutes, plus 30 minutes' soaking
cook 1 hour 20 minutes
serves 4

chicken mole poblano

ingredients

3 tbsp olive oil

4 chicken pieces, about 6 oz/175 g each, halved

1 onion, chopped

2 garlic cloves, finely chopped

1 hot dried red chili, such as chipotle, or 2 milder dried chilies, such as ancho, reconstituted following the package instructions and finely chopped

1 tbsp sesame seeds, toasted, plus extra to garnish

1 tbsp chopped almonds

¼ tsp each ground cinnamon, cumin, and cloves

3 tomatoes, peeled and chopped

2 tbsp raisins

1½ cups chicken stock

1 tbsp peanut butter

1 oz/25 g semisweet chocolate with a high cocoa content, grated, plus extra to garnish

fresh red chilies, sliced, to garnish

salt and pepper

To serve

Spicy Rice (optional)

Refried Beans and Pico de Gallo Salsa (optional)

one Heat 2 tablespoons of the oil in a large skillet. Add the chicken and cook until browned on all sides. Remove the chicken pieces with a slotted spoon and set aside.

two Add the onion, garlic, and chilies and cook for 5 minutes, or until softened. Add the sesame seeds, almonds, and spices and cook, stirring, for 2 minutes. Add the tomatoes, raisins, stock, peanut butter, and chocolate and stir well. Season to taste with salt and pepper and let simmer for 5 minutes.

three Transfer the mixture to a food processor or blender and process until smooth (you may need to do this in batches).

four Return the mixture to the skillet, add the chicken, and bring to a boil. Reduce the heat, cover, and let simmer for 1 hour, or until the chicken is very tender, adding more liquid if necessary.

five Garnish with sesame seeds, slices of fresh red chilies, and a little grated chocolate and serve with either Spicy Rice, to add color and texture, or some Refried Beans and Pico de Gallo Salsa.

The secret of fajita success lies in the marinating of the meat prior to quick cooking. It may take a little forward planning but the result is far superior.

prepare 15 minutes, plus 2–3 hours' marinating
cook 12–15 minutes
serves 4

chicken fajitas

ingredients

4 skinless, boneless chicken breasts
2 red bell peppers, seeded and cut into
  1-inch/2.5-cm strips
8 Flour Tortillas, warmed
Guacamole
sour cream
Pico de Gallo Salsa
shredded iceberg lettuce

Marinade
3 tbsp olive oil, plus extra for drizzling
3 tbsp maple syrup or honey
1 tbsp red wine vinegar
2 garlic cloves, crushed
2 tsp dried oregano
1–2 tsp dried red pepper flakes
salt and pepper

To serve
Refried Beans (optional)
Spicy Rice (optional)

one To make the marinade, place the oil, maple syrup, vinegar, garlic, oregano, pepper flakes, and salt and pepper to taste in a large, shallow dish or bowl and mix together.

two Slice the chicken across the grain into slices 1 inch/2.5 cm thick. Toss in the marinade until well coated. Cover and let chill in the refrigerator for 2–3 hours, turning occasionally.

three Heat a grill pan until hot. Lift the chicken slices from the marinade with a slotted spoon, lay on the grill pan, and cook over medium-high heat for 3–4 minutes on each side until cooked through. Remove the chicken to a warmed serving plate and keep warm.

four Add the bell peppers, skin-side down, to the grill pan and cook for 2 minutes on each side. Transfer to the serving plate.

five Pile the cooked chicken and bell peppers onto the warmed tortillas, along with some Guacamole, sour cream, Pico de Gallo Salsa, and some shredded iceberg lettuce. Serve with Refried Beans or Spicy Rice.

Chicken wings cooked in a wonderfully sticky, slightly spicy sauce never fail to please. You can serve the wings hot or warm.

prepare 10 minutes
cook 40–45 minutes
makes 12

san francisco wings

ingredients

5 tbsp dark soy sauce

2 tbsp dry sherry

1 tbsp rice vinegar

juice of 1 orange and 2-inch/5-cm strip of orange rind, pith removed

1 tbsp light muscovado sugar

1 star anise

1 orange

1 tsp cornstarch, mixed to a paste with 3 tbsp water

1 tbsp finely chopped fresh gingerroot

1 tsp chili sauce

3 lb 5 oz/1.5 kg chicken wings

one Preheat the oven to 400°F/200°C. Place the soy sauce, sherry, vinegar, orange rind, sugar, and star anise into a pan, and the juice extracted from the orange and mix well. Bring to a boil over medium heat, then stir in the cornstarch paste. Continue to boil, stirring constantly, for 1 minute, or until thickened. Remove the pan from the heat and stir in the ginger and chili sauce.

two Remove and discard the tips from the chicken wings and place the wings in a single layer in an ovenproof dish or roasting pan. Pour the sauce over the wings, turning and stirring to coat.

three Bake in the oven for 35–40 minutes, turning and basting with the sauce occasionally, until the chicken is tender and browned and the juices run clear when a skewer is inserted into the thickest part of the meat. Serve either hot or warm.

Thanksgiving isn't complete without a roast turkey at the center of the table, but don't let that put you off cooking this recipe at other times of the year. To save time, you can use a store-bought dressing, but for special occasions nothing can beat a homemade dressing.

prepare 20 minutes
cook 3½ hours
serves 8

traditional roast turkey

ingredients

1 turkey, weighing 11 lb/5 kg
4 tbsp butter
5 tbsp red wine
1¾ cups chicken stock
1 tbsp cornstarch
1 tsp French mustard
1 tsp sherry vinegar
2 tsp water

To serve
freshly cooked seasonal vegetables
dressing of your choice

one Preheat the oven to 425°F/220°C. Spoon the dressing into the neck cavity of the turkey and close the flap of skin with a skewer. Place the bird in a large roasting pan and rub all over with 3 tablespoons of the butter. Roast for 1 hour, then lower the oven temperature to 350°F/180°C and roast for an additional 2½ hours. You may need to pour off the fat from the roasting pan occasionally.

two Check that the turkey is cooked by inserting a skewer or the point of a sharp knife into the thigh; if the juices run clear, it is ready. Transfer the bird to a carving board, cover loosely with foil, and let rest.

three To make the gravy, skim off the fat from the roasting pan then place the pan over medium heat. Add the red wine and stir with a wooden spoon, scraping up the sediment from the bottom of the pan. Stir in the chicken stock. Mix the cornstarch, mustard, vinegar, and water together in a small bowl, then stir into the wine and stock. Bring to a boil, stirring constantly until thickened and smooth. Stir in the remaining butter.

four Carve the turkey and serve with vegetables, the dressing, and the gravy.

Grilling gives lobsters a lovely smoky scent that is enhanced by spicy red chili. Serve with creamy Refried Beans and a stack of warm corn tortillas.

lobster cooked beach style

ingredients

2–4 cooked lobsters, depending on their
  size, cut through the middle into two
  halves, or 4 lobster tails, the meat
  loosened slightly from its shell

Chili butter

½ cup unsalted butter, softened
3–4 tbsp chopped fresh cilantro
about 5 garlic cloves, chopped
2–3 tbsp mild chili powder
juice of 1 lime
salt and pepper

To serve

2½ cups Refried Beans
chopped scallions
lime wedges
salsa of your choice

cook's tip

The flavored butter is also
delicious with grilled fish
steaks and large shrimp.

one To make the chili butter, put the butter in a bowl and mix in the cilantro, garlic, chili powder, and lime juice. Add salt and pepper to taste.

two Rub the chili butter into the cut side of the lobster or the lobster tails, working it into all the lobsters' cracks and crevices.

three Wrap loosely in aluminum foil and place, cut-side up, on a rack over the hot coals of a barbecue. Cook for 15 minutes, or until heated through.

four Serve with Refried Beans, topped with chopped scallions, plus lime wedges and salsa.

Warm waters in the Gulf of Mexico are ideal for red snapper, making it a popular fish with fishermen and cooks alike. This recipe teams the snapper's tender, mild flesh with fresh orange juice.

prepare 20 minutes
cook 35 minutes
serves 4

stuffed red snapper

ingredients

1 red snapper, weighing 2 lb 4 oz/1 kg,
   cleaned, scaled, rinsed, and patted dry
lemon or orange wedges, to serve
salt and pepper

Orange basting sauce

generous ¼ cup corn oil
2 tbsp butter, melted
3 tbsp freshly squeezed orange juice
2 tbsp Worcestershire sauce
hot pepper sauce, to taste
salt and pepper

Citrus-shrimp stuffing

2 tbsp butter or 2 tbsp corn oil
2 tbsp red onion, minced
1 celery stalk, minced
½ cup fine dried white bread crumbs
3 oz/85 g cooked shelled shrimp, chopped
1½ oz/40 g cooked fresh crabmeat, picked
   over, or thawed and patted dry if frozen
2 tbsp chopped fresh parsley
½ tsp dried thyme or tarragon
finely grated rind and juice of 1 large orange
salt and pepper

one Preheat the oven to 350°F/180°C. To make the basting sauce, put all the ingredients into a jar with a tightly fitting lid and shake until blended. Set aside.

two To make the stuffing, melt the butter in a skillet over medium heat. Add the onion and celery and cook, stirring frequently, for 3–5 minutes until they are soft but not brown. Stir in the bread crumbs, shrimp, crabmeat, parsley, thyme, and orange rind. Slowly stir in the orange juice just until the stuffing is well blended. Add salt and pepper to taste.

three Season the red snapper's cavity with salt and pepper. Spoon in the stuffing and use wooden toothpicks to close the cavity and hold the stuffing in. Lay the fish in a roasting pan and pour over the basting sauce. Bake in the oven, basting once or twice, for 30 minutes, or until the fish is cooked through and the flesh flakes easily. Let rest for 2–3 minutes, then transfer the fish to a warmed serving platter, with lemon wedges for squeezing over.

cook's tip

Red snapper, also called Florida snapper, is easy to spot on the fish counter—it is dark red on top, fading to a more rosy red at the belly, with a silver sheen. If you can't find red snapper, this citrus-flavored stuffing also works well with sea bass.

When southerners talk about "fried fish," the chances are they are
referring to catfish, a bottom-feeding freshwater fish. Small, makeshift-
looking restaurants all along the Mississippi River pan-fry catfish with a
crispy cornmeal coating.

prepare 10 minutes
cook 4–8 minutes,
depending on the
size of your pan
serves 4

fried catfish fillets

ingredients

½ cup all-purpose flour

2 eggs

1½ cups yellow cornmeal

½ tsp dried thyme

pinch of cayenne pepper

2 lb/900 g catfish fillets, skinned, rinsed,
and patted dry

corn oil, for pan-frying

salt and pepper

To serve

Hush Puppies

Coleslaw

one Put the flour onto a plate. Beat the eggs in a wide, shallow bowl. Put the cornmeal onto
a separate plate and season with the thyme, cayenne pepper, and salt and pepper to taste.

two Dust the catfish fillets with the seasoned flour on both sides, shaking off any excess,
and dip into the eggs, then pat the cornmeal onto both sides.

three Heat about 2 inches/5 cm of oil in a large skillet over medium heat. Add as many
catfish fillets as will fit without overcrowding the skillet and cook for 2 minutes, or until the
coating is golden brown.

four Turn the catfish fillets over and cook for an additional 2 minutes, or until the flesh
flakes easily. Remove from the skillet with a slotted spoon and drain on paper towels.
Transfer the fillets to a low oven to keep warm while cooking the remaining fillets, if
necessary. Add more oil to the skillet as needed.

five For a true southern meal, serve the fried catfish with Hush Puppies and Coleslaw.
French Fries are another popular accompaniment.

variation

*Not many years ago, catfish was rarely
available outside the South, and was
an acquired taste. But now, catfish
farming is big business in Mississippi,
Louisiana, and Alabama, so catfish is
widely available and with less of a
"muddy" taste. If you can't find any
catfish, substitute river trout fillets.*

Virginian cooks along the Chesapeake Bay and Atlantic coast are renowned for their light, delicate crab cakes pan-fried in butter. Only a small amount of mayonnaise binds the ingredients, so allow plenty of chilling time, which makes handling easier.

prepare 15 minutes, plus 1¼ hours' chilling
cook 6–12 minutes, depending on the size of your pan
makes 8

chesapeake crab cakes

ingredients

3 eggs

2 scallions, finely chopped

3 tbsp mayonnaise

1 tbsp Dijon mustard

1 tbsp bottled grated horseradish

1 tbsp bottled capers, rinsed, drained, and chopped

1 tbsp chopped fresh parsley

½ tsp salt

¼ tsp pepper

pinch of cayenne pepper, or to taste

1 lb/450 g cooked fresh crabmeat, picked over, or thawed and patted dry if frozen

½ cup milk

½ cup all-purpose flour

2 cups fine dried white bread crumbs

up to 4 tbsp butter, for pan-frying

corn oil, for pan-frying

lime wedges, to serve

one Combine one of the eggs, the scallions, mayonnaise, mustard, horseradish, capers, parsley, salt, pepper, and cayenne pepper in a bowl and beat together. Stir in the crabmeat, then cover and chill for at least 30 minutes.

two Meanwhile, beat the remaining eggs with the milk in a wide, shallow bowl. Put the flour and bread crumbs onto separate plates. With wet hands, shape the crabmeat mixture into 8 equal balls and form into patties about 1-inch/2.5-cm thick. If the crab cakes feel too soft to hold their shape, return them to the refrigerator for 15 minutes, otherwise proceed with the next step.

three Lightly dust a crab cake with flour on both sides. Dip into the egg mixture, then pat the bread crumbs onto both sides. Continue until all the crab cakes are coated. Cover them and let chill for at least 45 minutes.

four Melt 2 tablespoons of the butter with ½ inch/1 cm of oil in a large skillet over medium heat. Add as many crab cakes as will fit without overcrowding the skillet and cook for 3 minutes on each side, or until golden brown and crisp.

five Remove the crab cakes from the skillet with a slotted spoon and drain on paper towels. Transfer to a low oven to keep warm while cooking the remaining crab cakes. Add more butter and oil to the skillet as needed. When all the crab cakes are cooked, serve with lime wedges.

Roasting the bell peppers, tomatoes, chilies, and garlic enhances the flavor of this sumptuous seafood medley. You can use any other firm fish fillets or a mixture, if you prefer.

prepare 20 minutes, plus 10 minutes' cooling
cook 50 minutes
serves 4

southwestern seafood stew

ingredients

1 each of yellow, red, and orange bell peppers, cored, seeded, and quartered

1 lb/450 g ripe tomatoes

2 large fresh mild green chilies, such as poblano

6 garlic cloves, peeled

2 tsp dried oregano or dried mixed herbs

2 tbsp olive oil, plus extra for drizzling

1 large onion, finely chopped

2 cups fish, vegetable, or chicken stock

finely grated rind and juice of 1 lime

2 tbsp chopped fresh cilantro, plus extra to garnish

1 bay leaf

1 lb/450 g red snapper fillets, skinned and cut into chunks

8 oz/225 g raw shrimp, shelled

8 oz/225 g cleaned squid, cut into rings

salt and pepper

warmed Flour Tortillas, to serve

one Preheat the oven to 400°F/200°C. Place the bell pepper quarters skin side up in a roasting pan with the tomatoes, chilies, and garlic. Sprinkle with the dried oregano and drizzle with oil. Roast in the oven for 30 minutes, or until the bell peppers are well browned and softened.

two Remove the roasted vegetables from the oven and let stand until cool enough to handle. Peel off the skins from the bell peppers, tomatoes, and chilies and chop the flesh. Finely chop the garlic.

three Heat the oil in a large pan. Add the onion and cook for 5 minutes, or until softened. Add the bell peppers, tomatoes, chilies, garlic, stock, lime rind and juice, chopped cilantro, bay leaf, and salt and pepper to taste. Bring to a boil, then stir in the seafood. Reduce the heat, cover, and let simmer gently for 10 minutes, or until the seafood is just cooked through. Discard the bay leaf, then garnish with chopped cilantro before serving with warmed Flour Tortillas.

Ever since canned condensed soups were invented in the United States in 1897, they have been used in casserole cooking. The most popular of these meals from the pantry continues to be tuna-noodle casserole.

prepare 20 minutes
cook 30–35 minutes
serves 4–6

tuna-noodle casserole

ingredients

7 oz/200 g dried egg ribbon pasta, such as tagliatelle

2 tbsp butter

2 oz/55 g fine fresh bread crumbs

1¼ cups condensed canned cream of mushroom soup

4 fl oz/125 ml milk

2 celery stalks, chopped

1 red and 1 green bell pepper, cored, seeded and chopped

5 oz/140 g mature Cheddar cheese, coarsely grated

2 tbsp chopped fresh parsley

7 oz/200 g canned tuna in oil, drained and flaked

salt and pepper

one Preheat the oven to 400°F/200°C. Bring a large pan of salted water to a boil. Add the pasta and cook for 2 minutes less than specified on the package instructions.

two Meanwhile, melt the butter in a separate, small pan over medium heat. Stir in the bread crumbs, then remove from the heat and set aside.

three Drain the pasta well and set aside. Pour the soup into the pasta pan over medium heat, then stir in the milk, celery, bell peppers, half the cheese, and the parsley. Add the tuna and gently stir in so that the flakes don't break up. Season to taste with salt and pepper. Heat just until small bubbles appear around the edge of the mixture—do not boil.

four Stir the pasta into the pan and use 2 forks to mix all the ingredients together. Spoon the mixture into an ovenproof dish that is also suitable for serving, and spread out.

five Stir the remaining cheese into the buttered bread crumbs, then sprinkle over the top of the pasta mixture. Bake in the oven for 20–25 minutes until the topping is golden. Let stand for 5 minutes before serving straight from the dish.

did you know?

When Dr. J. T. Dorrance invented condensed soup for the Campbell Soup Company, he probably never imagined the influence that it would have on American cooking. The company estimates that at the beginning of 21st century, 40 million cans of condensed soup were used in family favorites, such as this dish, during the course of a year.

Boston has been described as "the home of the bean and the cod."—It may not be a glamorous association, but this unusual fish pie demonstrates that it is a tasty and filling combination.

prepare 15 minutes
cook 40 minutes
serves 6

boston fish pie

ingredients

2 tbsp butter, plus extra for greasing

2 onions, chopped

2 lb 4 oz/1 kg cod fillet, skinned and cut
   into strips

4 rindless lean bacon strips, cut into
   1¼ x ½-inch/3 x 1-cm lengths

2 tbsp chopped fresh parsley

14 oz/400 g canned great northern beans,
   drained and rinsed

2½ cups milk

1 lb 2 oz/500 g potatoes, very thinly sliced

salt and pepper

fresh parsley sprigs, to garnish

variation

You could use an equal mixture of
fresh and smoked cod and add a few
juniper berries with the parsley, if you
would like a stronger flavor.

one Preheat the oven to 350°F/180°C. Lightly grease a flameproof casserole with a little butter. Arrange the onions in the bottom and cover with the strips of fish and bacon. Sprinkle with the parsley and season to taste with salt and pepper.

two Add the great northern beans, then pour in the milk. Arrange the potato slices, overlapping them slightly, to cover the entire surface of the pie.

three Dot the potato slices with the butter. Bake the pie in the oven for 40 minutes, or until the potatoes are crisp and golden. Garnish with parsley sprigs and serve immediately.

This is a gourmet, not to say healthy take on a trusty southwestern favorite—ideal for an informal dinner party. Use cooked shrimp and just heat through gently in the sauce for an everyday option.

prepare 20 minutes
cook 35 minutes
serves 4

chili-shrimp tacos

ingredients

1 lb 5 oz/600 g raw shrimp, shelled

2 tbsp chopped fresh flat-leaf parsley

12 tortilla shells

sour cream

chopped scallions, to garnish

Taco sauce

1 tbsp olive oil

1 onion, finely chopped

1 green bell pepper, cored, seeded
and diced

1–2 fresh hot green chilies, such
as jalapeño, seeded and finely chopped

3 garlic cloves, crushed

1 tsp ground cumin

1 tsp ground coriander

1 tsp brown sugar

1 lb/450 g ripe tomatoes, peeled
and coarsely chopped

juice of ½ lemon

salt and pepper

To serve

Pico de Gallo Salsa

Broiled Bell Pepper Relish

one Preheat the oven to 350°F/180°C. To make the sauce, heat the oil in a deep skillet over medium heat. Add the onion and cook for 5 minutes, or until softened. Add the bell pepper and chilies and cook for 5 minutes. Add the garlic, cumin, coriander, and sugar and cook the sauce for an additional 2 minutes, stirring.

two Add the tomatoes, lemon juice, and salt and pepper to taste. Bring to a boil, then reduce the heat and let simmer for 10 minutes.

three Stir in the shrimp and parsley, cover, and cook gently for 5–8 minutes until the shrimp are pink and tender.

four Meanwhile, place the tortilla shells, open-side down, on a baking sheet. Warm in the oven for 2–3 minutes.

five To serve, spoon the shrimp mixture into the tortilla shells, top with a spoonful of sour cream, and garnish with chopped scallions. Serve with Pico de Gallo Salsa and some Broiled Bell Pepper Relish.

Make a change from the standard pizza toppings—this dish is piled high with seafood and baked with a delicious broiled red bell pepper and tomato sauce. Serve with a crisp salad for a delicious light lunch.

prepare 25 minutes, plus 1 hour's rising
cook 55 minutes
serves 4

seafood pizza

ingredients

5 oz/140 g standard pizza base mix
4 tbsp chopped fresh dill or 2 tbsp
   dried dill
fresh dill, to garnish

Sauce
1 large red bell pepper, cored, seeded,
   and halved
14 oz/400 g canned chopped tomatoes
   with onion and herbs
3 tbsp tomato paste
salt and pepper

Topping
12 oz/350 g assorted cooked seafood,
   thawed if frozen
1 tbsp capers in brine, drained
2 tbsp pitted black olives in brine, drained
1 oz/25 g mozzarella cheese, grated
1 tbsp freshly grated Parmesan cheese

cook's tip

To make peeling the bell peppers easier, place them in a plastic bag after blackening their skins under the broiler, and let cool.

one Place the pizza base mix in a large bowl and stir in the dill. Make the dough according to the package instructions.

two Press the dough into a circle measuring 10 inches/25 cm across on a baking sheet lined with parchment paper. Let rise for 1 hour until doubled in size.

three Preheat the oven to 400°F/200°C. Preheat the broiler to hot. To make the sauce, arrange the bell pepper halves on a broiler rack. Cook under the preheated hot broiler for 8–10 minutes until the flesh is soft and the skin is blackened and blistered. Let cool slightly, then peel off the skin, chop the flesh, and place in a pan with the tomatoes. Bring to a boil and let simmer for 10 minutes. Stir in the tomato paste and season to taste with salt and pepper.

four Spread the sauce over the pizza base and top with the seafood. Sprinkle over the capers and olives, top with the cheeses, and bake in the oven for 25–30 minutes. Garnish with sprigs of dill and serve hot, cut into slices.

These crisp deep-fried packages are universally appealing and are speedy to make. For an alternative meat filling, try the Lone Star Chili topped with chopped onion and grated cheese. Enjoy this feast with a tequila.

prepare 20 minutes
cook 35 minutes
serves 4

spinach and mushroom chimichangas

ingredients

2 tbsp olive oil

1 large onion, finely chopped

8 oz/225 g small mushrooms, finely sliced

2 fresh mild green chilies, seeded and finely chopped

2 garlic cloves, finely chopped

5½ cups spinach leaves, torn into pieces if large

6 oz/175 g Cheddar cheese, grated

8 Flour Tortillas, warmed

vegetable oil, for deep-frying

To serve

Guacamole

sour cream

tomatoes, seeded and chopped

onions, chopped

Spicy Rice

one Heat the oil in a large, heavy-bottom skillet. Add the onion and cook over medium heat for 5 minutes, or until softened.

two Add the mushrooms, chilies, and garlic and cook for 5 minutes, or until the mushrooms are lightly browned. Add the spinach and cook, stirring, for 1–2 minutes until just wilted. Add the cheese and stir until just melted.

three Spoon an equal quantity of the mixture into the center of each tortilla. Fold in the opposite sides of each tortilla to cover the filling, then roll up to enclose it completely.

four Heat the oil for deep-frying in a deep-fryer or large, deep pan to 350–375°F/180–190°C, or until a cube of bread browns in 30 seconds. Deep-fry the chimichangas two at a time, turning once, for 5–6 minutes until crisp and golden. Drain on paper towels before serving with a spoonful of Guacamole and sour cream, some chopped tomatoes and onion, and a side dish of Spicy Rice.

accompaniments

The word "bread" in the title of this southern classic is a misnomer, as the texture is more like a cornmeal soufflé or pudding. Its name might be derived from the Native American word for porridge, *suppawn*, or simply be a reference to the spoon used to serve it straight from the baking dish.

prepare 10 minutes, plus 15 minutes' cooling
cook 40–45 minutes
serves 4–6

spoon bread

ingredients

2 cups yellow cornmeal
1½ tsp salt
2 tbsp butter, plus extra for greasing
   and to serve (optional)
2½ cups boiling water
2 eggs, separated
1 tsp baking soda
1½ cups buttermilk

did you know?

Southern cooks prefer to make spoon bread with white cornmeal, but as it is rarely sold outside the region, yellow cornmeal is used in most recipes. In colonial days, spoon bread took the place of bread made with refined white flour, which was prohibitively expensive for all but the wealthiest.

one Preheat the oven to 425°F/220°C. Grease a 1½-quart/1.7-liter baking dish, which is also suitable for serving.

two Stir the cornmeal and salt together in a heatproof bowl. Add the butter and boiling water and stir until the mixture is smooth, then set it aside to cool slightly.

three Stir the egg yolks into the cornmeal mixture. Stir the baking soda into the buttermilk in a pitcher until dissolved, then stir into the cornmeal mixture to make a thin, smooth batter.

four Using an electric mixer, beat the egg whites in a separate bowl until stiff peaks form. Beat a large spoonful of the egg whites into the cornmeal batter to lighten, then fold in the remaining egg whites.

five Spoon the batter into the prepared dish and bake in the oven for 40–45 minutes until the top is set and golden brown. Serve straight from the dish while the spoon bread is hot, with plenty of butter to melt over the top of each portion.

Fresh, homemade flour tortillas are, unsurprisingly, rather more delicious than the store-bought variety. As well as playing a leading role in many southwestern mainstays, flour tortillas are great with soups and stews such as Beef and Pea Soup, Southwestern Seafood Stew, and Lone Star Chili.

prepare 40 minutes, plus 15 minutes' resting
cook 24–48 minutes
makes 12

flour tortillas

ingredients

2¼ cups all-purpose flour, plus extra
   for dusting
1 tsp salt
½ tsp baking powder
6 tbsp shortening or white vegetable fat,
   diced
about ½ cup hot water

one Sift the flour, salt, and baking powder into a large bowl. Add the shortening and rub it in with your fingertips until the mixture resembles fine bread crumbs. Add enough water to form a soft dough.

two Turn out the dough onto a lightly floured counter and knead until smooth. Divide the dough into 12 pieces and shape each into a ball. Cover with a clean dish towel and let rest for 15 minutes.

three Roll out 1 ball at a time into a 7-inch/18-cm circle, keeping the remainder of the dough covered. Stack the tortillas between sheets of nonstick parchment paper.

four Heat a grill pan or large, heavy-bottom skillet over medium-high heat. Cook 1 tortilla at a time for 1–2 minutes on each side until lightly browned in places and puffed up. Serve warm.

Few pan-fried catfish dinners in the South are served without a portion of these golden, deep-fried cornmeal dumplings on the side. Traditionally, they are cooked in the pan that the catfish was fried in, using the same fat for extra flavor.

prepare 10 minutes
cook 15 minutes
makes about 36

hush puppies

ingredients

1¾ cups yellow cornmeal
½ cup all-purpose flour, sifted
1 small onion, finely chopped
1 tbsp superfine sugar
2 tsp baking powder
½ tsp salt
¾ cup milk
1 egg, beaten
corn oil, for deep-frying

one Stir the cornmeal, flour, onion, sugar, baking powder, and salt together in a bowl and make a well in the center.

two Beat the milk and egg together in a pitcher, then pour into the dry ingredients and stir until a thick batter forms.

three Heat at least 2 inches/5 cm of oil in a deep skillet or pan over high heat until the temperature reaches 350–375°F/180–190°C, or until a cube of bread browns in 30 seconds.

four Drop in as many teaspoonfuls of the batter as will fit without overcrowding the skillet and cook, stirring constantly, until the Hush Puppies puff up and turn golden.

five Remove the Hush Puppies from the oil with a slotted spoon and drain on paper towels. Reheat the oil, if necessary, and cook the remaining batter. Serve hot.

did you know?

It is said that Hush Puppies were given their name in the days before indoor kitchens. Busy, harassed cooks would cook cornmeal mush and toss it to begging and yelping dogs with the words, "Hush, puppy!"

Frijoles refritos, to give them their proper name, are a southwestern must and, while you can depend on the canned variety, why not enjoy the real thing now and again? You can ladle these, without the cheese, on the side of many of the main courses in this book, such as Chicken Mole Poblano or Beef Enchiladas.

prepare 10 minutes,
plus 8 hours' soaking
cook 2¼ hours
serves 4

refried beans

ingredients

1½ cups dried pinto beans, soaked
   overnight
2 onions, 1 quartered and 1 chopped
2 bay leaves, 1 chopped and 1 whole
1 fresh thyme sprig
1 dried red chili, such as ancho
3 tbsp olive oil
2 tsp ground cumin
3 oz/85 g Cheddar cheese, grated
   (optional)

one Drain the beans, rinse under cold running water, and place in a large pan with the quartered onion, the herbs, and chili. Pour over enough cold water to cover and bring to a boil. Reduce the heat, cover, and let simmer gently for 2 hours, or until the beans are very tender.

two Drain the beans, reserving the cooking liquid, and discard the onion, herbs, and chili.

three Place two-thirds of the beans with the cooking liquid in a food processor or blender and process until coarsely blended.

four Heat the oil in a heavy-bottom skillet over medium heat. Add the chopped onion and cook for 10 minutes, or until soft and golden. Add the cumin and cook, stirring, for 2 minutes. Stir in the puréed and reserved beans and cook, stirring constantly, until the liquid reduces and the mixture thickens. Stir in the grated cheese, if using, and cook, stirring, until melted. Serve immediately.

Don't let the title of this Cajun dish from the Louisiana backwaters put you off—"dirty" simply refers to the dusty brown color of the rice when it is combined with the stewed chicken livers.

prepare 15 minutes
cook 45 minutes
serves 4–6 as a side dish;
2–3 as a main course

dirty rice

ingredients

2 tbsp rendered bacon fat or corn oil

2 tbsp all-purpose flour

2 large garlic cloves, minced

1 onion, finely chopped

1 celery stalk, finely chopped

½ green bell pepper, cored, seeded, and finely chopped

4 tbsp finely chopped fresh parsley

1 lb/450 g chicken livers, thawed if frozen, trimmed, and chopped

½ tsp Worcestershire sauce

pinch of cayenne pepper, or to taste

½ cup chicken or vegetable stock

1 cup long-grain rice

6 scallions, finely chopped

salt and pepper

hot pepper sauce, to serve

one Heat the bacon fat in a large skillet over medium-high heat for 1–2 minutes. Reduce the heat to medium-low, sprinkle in the flour, and stir to make a smooth paste, or roux. Stir constantly for 20 minutes, or until the roux turns a golden brown color.

two Stir in the garlic, onion, celery, bell pepper, and parsley and cook, stirring frequently, for 2–3 minutes until the vegetables are softened. Add the chicken livers, Worcestershire sauce, cayenne pepper, and salt and pepper to taste and cook, stirring constantly with a wooden spoon to break down the livers, for 5 minutes.

three Add the stock and bring to a boil, stirring constantly. Reduce the heat to low and let simmer, uncovered, for 15 minutes, stirring occasionally.

four Meanwhile, cook the rice in a pan of lightly salted boiling water until it is light and fluffy. Drain well and keep warm until the chicken livers and vegetables are cooked.

five Stir the rice and scallions into the liver mixture and adjust the seasoning. Serve immediately, with a bottle of hot pepper sauce on the side.

did you know?

Cajun cooking is country cooking, unlike the more refined Creole cooking of the cities. Cajun cooks, generally poor and thrifty, made creative use of every part of an animal, and traditional recipes for this dish include chicken gizzards as well as livers.

Full of both color and flavor, this is so much more inviting than plain boiled rice. Add some canned red kidney or black-eye peas with the stock for a more substantial alternative. Serve as an accompaniment to Spinach and Mushroom Chimichangas, or Refried Beans and Chicken Fajitas.

prepare 15 minutes, plus 5 minutes' standing
cook 30 minutes
serves 4

spicy rice

ingredients

1 fresh corncob
3 tbsp olive oil
6 scallions, chopped
1 celery stalk, finely chopped
3 garlic cloves, finely chopped
2 green bell peppers, cored, seeded, and chopped
2 fresh mild green chilies, seeded and finely chopped

generous 1 1/4 cups long-grain rice
2 tsp ground cumin
2 1/2 cups chicken or vegetable stock
2 tbsp chopped fresh cilantro
salt and pepper
fresh cilantro sprigs, to garnish

one Cut the corn from the corncob. Heat the oil in a large, heavy-bottom pan over medium heat. Add the scallions, celery, and garlic and cook for 5 minutes, or until softened. Add the bell peppers, chilies, and corn and cook for 5 minutes.

two Add the rice and cumin and cook, stirring to coat the grains in the oil, for 2 minutes.

three Stir in the stock and half the chopped cilantro and bring to a boil. Reduce the heat, cover, and let simmer for 15 minutes, or until nearly all the liquid has been absorbed and the rice is just tender.

four Remove from the heat and fluff up with a fork. Stir in the remaining chopped cilantro and season to taste with salt and pepper. Let stand, covered, for 5 minutes before serving. Serve garnished with cilantro sprigs.

Black-eye peas—small, nut-brown, kidney-shaped peas with a black "eye"—are used in many soul-food and Cajun recipes. For a true taste of the Deep South, serve these as an accompaniment to broiled ribs or meat, with simmered greens and cornsticks.

prepare 15 minutes
cook 45–55 minutes
serves 4–6

a pot of southern peas

ingredients

8 oz/225 g boneless, rindless belly of
   pork, cut into ½-inch/1-cm strips
2 large garlic cloves, crushed
1 onion, finely chopped
1 red bell pepper, cored, seeded,
   and finely chopped
1 celery stalk, finely chopped
1 fresh red chili, seeded and chopped
4 large tomatoes, peeled, seeded,
   and chopped
1 cup water
1 lb 12 oz/800 g canned black-eye peas,
   drained and rinsed
1 tbsp blackstrap molasses
salt and pepper
hot pepper sauce, to serve

did you know?

Black-eye peas, called cowpeas in the South, are another staple ingredient brought from Africa via the slave trade. It is a long-standing southern tradition to eat black-eye peas on New Year's Day in Hoppin' John.

one Put the belly of pork into a deep, dry skillet or pan with a lid over medium-high heat and cook, stirring occasionally, for 10–15 minutes until brown and crisp. Remove the pork from the skillet with a slotted spoon and set aside. Pour off all but 1½–2 tablespoons of the rendered fat.

two Reduce the heat to medium, stir in the garlic and onion, and cook, stirring frequently, for 3–5 minutes until the onion is soft. Add the bell pepper, celery, and chili and cook, stirring occasionally, for an additional 3 minutes. Add the tomatoes, water, and pepper to taste and bring to a boil. Reduce the heat, cover, and let simmer for 20 minutes.

three Return the pork to the skillet with the peas and molasses and stir to dissolve the molasses. Let the peas simmer uncovered, stirring occasionally, for 10 minutes, or until most of the liquid has evaporated and the peas are hot. Season to taste with salt and pepper and serve with a bottle of hot pepper sauce on the side.

These are the original baked beans and you will find them much tastier than the canned variety. They were traditionally cooked with salt pork, but omitting the meat makes this dish suitable for vegetarians and vegans too.

prepare 10 minutes
cook 5½ hours
serves 8

boston beans

ingredients

1 lb 2 oz/500 g dried great northern beans,
   soaked overnight
2 onions, chopped
2 large tomatoes, peeled and chopped
2 tsp mustard
2 tbsp molasses
salt and pepper

one Preheat the oven to 275°F/140°C. Drain the beans, rinse under cold running water, and place in a large pan. Add enough cold water to cover, bring to a boil, then reduce the heat and simmer for 15 minutes. Drain, reserving 1¼ cups of the cooking liquid. Transfer the beans to a large casserole and add the onions.

two Return the reserved cooking liquid to the pan and add the tomatoes. Bring to a boil, then reduce the heat and simmer for 10 minutes. Remove from the heat, stir in the mustard and molasses, and season to taste with salt and pepper.

three Pour the mixture into the casserole and bake in the preheated oven for 5 hours. Serve hot.

variation

If you are a meat-eater and want to cook the original one-pot meal, add 12 oz/350 g diced salt pork to the casserole with the onions in Step 1.

French fries, pommes frites, or chips, from chunky to shoestring—call
them what you wish, but a simply broiled, grilled, or pan-fried steak
wouldn't be the same without this classic bistro accompaniment!

prepare 10 minutes,
plus 50 minutes' soaking
and cooling
cook 25–35 minutes
serves 4

french fries

ingredients

1 lb 8 oz/675 g large potatoes (see
Cook's Tip)
sunflower-seed, corn, or peanut oil,
for deep-frying
salt and pepper

one Peel the potatoes and cut into ⅜-inch/8-mm even-size fingers. As soon as they are
prepared, put them into a large bowl of cold water to prevent discoloration, then let them
soak for 30 minutes to remove the excess starch.

two Drain the potatoes and dry well on a clean dish towel. Heat the oil in a deep-fryer or
large, heavy-bottom pan to 375°F/190°C. If you do not have a thermometer, test the
temperature by dropping a potato finger into the oil. If it sinks, the oil isn't hot enough; if it
floats and the oil bubbles around the potato, it is ready. Carefully add a small batch of
potatoes to the oil (this is to ensure even cooking and to avoid reducing the temperature of
the oil) and deep-fry for 5–6 minutes until soft but not browned. Remove from the oil and
drain well on paper towels. Let cool for at least 5 minutes. Continue to deep-fry the
remaining potatoes in the same way, allowing the oil to return to the correct temperature
each time.

three When ready to serve, reheat the oil to 400°F/200°C. Add the potatoes, in small
batches, and deep-fry for 2–3 minutes until golden brown. Remove from the oil and drain on
paper towels. Serve immediately, seasoned to taste with salt and pepper.

cook's tip

The secret of making crisp, golden
fries is to cook the potatoes in small
batches, in two stages—in advance
and just before serving—and to use
a variety of potato that produces a
crisp outer shell with a fluffy, light
inside. Russet Burbank, Russet
Arcadia, California long whites,
and Butte are all suitable.

Potato wedges are a contemporary way of serving potatoes. Here they are spiced, according to your taste, for serving as an accompaniment, but they are equally good served as a snack (see Variation).

prepare 10 minutes
cook 40–45 minutes
serves 4

spicy potato wedges

ingredients

1 lb 8 oz/675 g large, firm potatoes, such
    as round white, round red, Yukon gold,
    or russet
3 tbsp vegetable oil
1 tbsp paprika or 2 tsp ground coriander
1 tsp each cumin seeds and turmeric
salt and pepper
chopped fresh cilantro, to garnish

variation

To serve as a snack, sprinkle the cooked potato wedges with grated cheese, cook them under a preheated medium broiler until the cheese is melted and bubbling, and serve with a tomato salsa or dipping sauce, or simply with a bowl of sour cream and chives.

one Preheat the oven to 400°F/200°C. Scrub the potatoes, then cut each in half lengthwise and then in half again until you have 8 even-shaped wedges. Put into a large pan of salted water, bring to a boil, and boil for 3 minutes. Drain well and return the wedges to the pan.

two Add the oil to the pan and toss the potato wedges in it until coated. Add the paprika, cumin seeds, and turmeric, season to taste with salt and pepper, and mix well together.

three Spread the potato wedges out on a baking sheet and bake in the oven for 35–40 minutes until tender and golden brown, turning 2–3 times during cooking. Serve hot, sprinkled with chopped cilantro to garnish.

Recipes for Hashed Brown Potatoes vary greatly from region to region. They might use grated raw, cubed raw, or cooked potatoes, but whichever you use, there is no comparison between a homecooked and a store-bought, frozen variety!

prepare 15 minutes,
plus 15 minutes' draining
cook 25 minutes
serves 3–4

hashed brown potatoes

ingredients

4 large potatoes
1 small onion, finely chopped (optional)
1 large tbsp butter
vegetable oil, for pan-frying
salt and pepper
fresh flat-leaf parsley sprigs, to garnish

one Peel, then coarsely grate the potatoes. Put into a strainer and rinse under cold running water, then let drain for about 15 minutes. Using the back of a wooden spoon, push out any excess water, then wrap the potatoes in a clean dish towel and dry very thoroughly.

two Put the potatoes into a large bowl. Add the onion, if using, season to taste with salt and pepper, and mix well together.

three Melt the butter with a generous film of oil in a large, heavy-bottom skillet over medium heat. When hot, add the potatoes and toss them several times in the butter and oil, then press down with a spatula and spread evenly over the bottom of the skillet. Press down firmly again. Reduce the heat to low, cover, and cook for 10 minutes, or until the base of the pancake is crisp and golden brown. During cooking, press the pancake down several more times and gently shake the skillet to make sure it isn't sticking.

four Using a spatula, cut the pancake in 4 wedges, then carefully turn each wedge. If the bottom of the skillet appears too dry, add a little more oil to prevent the potatoes from sticking. Cook the second side, uncovered, for 15 minutes, or until tender and golden brown. Serve immediately.

variation

The potatoes in this recipe are cooked as one large, round pancake, but, if preferred, they can be cooked as individual pancakes in the same way.

Most Americans eat sweet potatoes just once a year with their Thanksgiving turkey, but for southerners, these orange-fleshed tubers are a more versatile everyday vegetable.

prepare 20 minutes
cook 35–45 minutes
serves 4–6

candied sweet potatoes

ingredients

3 large orange-fleshed sweet potatoes, about 9 oz/250 g each, scrubbed

2 tbsp butter, melted and cooled, plus extra for greasing

¼ cup brown sugar

finely grated rind of ½ orange

4 tbsp freshly squeezed orange juice

pinch of cayenne pepper, or to taste (optional)

one Bring a large pan of water to a boil over high heat. Add the sweet potatoes and cook for 15 minutes. Drain, then put them under cold running water to cool. When cool enough to handle, peel, then cut each into 8 wedges or chunks.

two Preheat the oven to 400°F/200°C. Lightly grease a baking dish large enough to hold all the wedges or chunks in a single layer, and add the part-cooked potatoes.

three Put the butter, sugar, and orange rind and juice into a small pan over medium heat and stir until the sugar dissolves. Bring to a boil and boil until the liquid reduces by about one-third. Stir in the cayenne pepper, if using.

four Generously brush the sweet potatoes with the glaze. Bake in the oven, glazing an additional 2–3 times at intervals, for 20–30 minutes until the sweet potatoes are tender when pierced with the tip of a knife or a skewer. These are excellent served hot, but are also delicious if left to cool and served as part of a picnic or barbecue spread.

cook's tip

Two varieties of sweet potato (Ipomoea batatas) are grown in the South—one with a pale yellow flesh and the other with a vibrant orange flesh. It is the orange-fleshed variety that you need for this dish. These are often referred to as "yams" by southerners, but true yams (Dioscorea bulbifera) are quite different.

These onions are coated in a thick batter and deep-fried until crisp and golden brown; for a lighter alternative, simply dip them in milk followed by seasoned flour before deep-frying.

prepare 15 minutes
cook 15 minutes
serves 4–6

crispy onion rings

ingredients

generous ¾ cup all-purpose flour
1 egg
⅔ cup lowfat milk
4 large onions
vegetable oil, for deep-frying
chili powder, to taste (optional)
salt and pepper
lettuce leaves, to serve

cook's tip

There are dozens of different methods that people claim can help to prevent you from crying while cutting onions, such as leaving the root intact until the very end, peeling them under running water, chilling them before cutting, and even whistling while you work!

one To make the batter, sift the flour and a pinch of salt into a large bowl and make a well in the center. Break the egg into the well and gently beat with a whisk. Gradually whisk in the milk, drawing the flour from the side into the liquid in the center to form a smooth batter.

two Leaving the onions whole, slice widthwise into ¼-inch/5-mm slices, then separate each slice into rings.

three Heat the oil in a deep-fryer or deep, heavy-bottom pan to 350–375°F/180–190°C, or until a cube of bread browns in 30 seconds.

four Using the tines of a fork, pick up several onions rings at a time and dip in the batter. Let any excess batter drip off, then add the onions to the oil and deep-fry for 1–2 minutes until they rise to the surface of the oil and become crisp and golden brown. Remove from the oil, drain on paper towels, and keep warm while deep-frying the remaining onion rings in batches. Do not try to deep-fry too many at a time, as this will reduce the temperature of the oil and the onion rings will absorb some of the oil and become soggy.

five Season the onion rings with chili powder, if wished, and salt and pepper to taste, then serve immediately on a bed of lettuce leaves.

These sweet, caramelized onions can be served as a hot vegetable accompaniment, or cold as a condiment with broiled, grilled, or pan-fried steak, burgers, or cold cooked meats. They can be prepared ahead and stored in the refrigerator for several days.

prepare 15 minutes
cook 1 hour 50 minutes
serves 4

sweet-and-sour glazed onions

ingredients

1 lb 8 oz/675 g pearl or pickling onions

4 tbsp butter

1 tbsp olive oil

1½ cups water

1 tbsp tomato paste

2 tbsp sugar

2 tbsp red wine vinegar

salt and pepper

one Peel the onions, but keep the root intact so that they do not fall apart during cooking. Melt the butter with the oil in a large, heavy-bottom skillet over medium heat, add the onions, and cook for 5 minutes, gently shaking the skillet occasionally.

two Add the water and tomato paste to the skillet and cook for 30 minutes, stirring frequently.

three Add the sugar and vinegar to the onions and season to taste with salt and pepper. Reduce the heat to low and cook for 1¼ hours, or until tender and golden brown. If the mixture shows signs of becoming too dry, add a little more water. Serve hot (see Variation) or cold.

variation

If serving hot as a vegetable accompaniment, 2 tablespoons of raisins or golden raisins can be added about 30 minutes before the end of cooking.

Stewed tomatoes are a traditional southern side dish, again with many variations. This sweet, baked recipe, with bread cubes to soak up the moisture of the tomatoes as they cook, is good for entertaining, as it can be assembled in advance, and ready for baking.

prepare 10 minutes
cook 40 minutes
serves 4–6

scalloped tomatoes

ingredients

1 lb 5 oz/600 g juicy, ripe tomatoes,
coarsely chopped

3½ oz/100 g fresh bread, cut into
¼-inch/5-mm cubes

4 scallions, finely chopped

1 tbsp tomato paste (optional)

4 tbsp butter, diced

½ cup brown sugar

snipped chives or chopped fresh parsley,
to garnish

one Preheat the oven to 400°F/200°C. Put the tomatoes, bread cubes, and scallions into a baking dish and gently toss together. If the tomatoes are not bright red, stir in the tomato paste.

two Scatter the diced butter over the surface and sprinkle with the sugar. Bake in the oven for 15 minutes. Give the tomatoes a good stir then bake for an additional 15 minutes.

three Increase the temperature to 425°F/220°C. Give the tomatoes a final stir and bake for an additional 10 minutes, or until the tomatoes are tender and the bread cubes are slightly caramelized. Sprinkle with the chives and serve hot.

did you know?

Scalloped tomatoes have been a part of southern dining for several hundred years. Preserved menus reveal that Thomas Jefferson served them in splendid meals at Monticello, his plantation on the banks of the Potomac River, in the late 18th century.

Lightly cooked zucchini are mixed here with ripe, juicy tomatoes and
dressed with a chili vinaigrette to create a perfect side salad.

prepare 10 minutes,
plus 20 minutes' standing
cook 20 minutes
serves 4–6

zucchini and tomato salad

ingredients

1 large fresh mild green chili, or a
   combination of 1 green bell pepper and
   ½–1 fresh green chili

4 zucchini, sliced

2–3 garlic cloves, finely chopped

pinch of superfine sugar

¼ tsp ground cumin

2 tbsp white wine vinegar

4 tbsp extra virgin olive oil

2–3 tbsp chopped fresh cilantro

4 ripe tomatoes, diced or sliced

salt and pepper

variation

To make this into a more substantial
dish, add 8 oz/225 g cooked peeled
shrimp to the salad before coating
with the dressing in Step 5.

one Fry the mild chili, or the combination of the bell pepper and chili, in a heavy-bottom
ungreased skillet or broil under a preheated broiler until the skin is charred. Place in a plastic
bag, twist to seal well, and leave the charred vegetable(s) to stand for 20 minutes.

two Peel the skin from the chili and bell pepper, if using, then carefully remove the seeds
and slice the flesh fairly thinly. Keep to one side.

three Bring about 2 inches/5 cm water to a boil in the bottom of a steamer. Add the
zucchini to the top part of the steamer, cover, and steam for about 5 minutes until just tender.
Let cool.

four Meanwhile, combine the garlic, sugar, cumin, vinegar, oil, and cilantro thoroughly in a
bowl. Stir in the chili and bell pepper, if using, then season with salt and pepper to taste.

five Arrange the zucchini and tomatoes in a serving bowl or on a platter and spoon over the
chili dressing. Serve the salad immediately.

Most Americans claim indifference to or dislike of okra, but in the South, this long, green, ridged pod is the star of many traditional soul-food recipes, as well as Creole and Cajun dishes. This is the recipe to win over anyone who claims to dislike okra's texture.

prepare 10 minutes
cook 10 minutes
serves 4–6

deep-fried okra

ingredients

1 lb/450 g fresh okra, trimmed and cut into ½-inch/1-cm thick slices

about 4 tbsp water

½ cup yellow cornmeal

3 tbsp self-rising or all-purpose flour

½ tsp salt

pepper

vegetable oil, for deep-frying

one Put the okra into a bowl, sprinkle over the water, and gently stir the okra to just moisten.

two Put the cornmeal, flour, salt, and pepper to taste into a plastic bag, hold closed, and shake to mix. Add the okra slices to the bag and shake until lightly coated—they won't become completely coated.

three Heat at least 2 inches/5 cm of oil in a deep skillet or pan over high heat until the temperature reaches 350–375°F/180–190°C, or until a cube of bread browns in 30 seconds. Add as many okra slices as will fit without overcrowding the skillet and cook, stirring occasionally, for 2 minutes, or until the okra is bright green and the cornmeal coating is golden yellow.

four Remove the okra from the oil with a slotted spoon and drain on paper towels. Reheat the oil, if necessary, and cook the remaining okra.

five Serve the okra slices hot as a side dish, or serve hot or cold as a snack.

cook's tip

Originally from Africa, okra is now grown throughout the region, with Georgia, Florida, and Texas growers supplying most of the nation. Okra's most distinctive characteristic is the slimy substance it gives off when cut and heated, which is used to thicken soups and stews. This deep-frying technique, however, keeps it crunchy.

Roasted root vegetables are particularly popular since they all cook together and need little attention once prepared. You can use whatever is available: potatoes, parsnips, turnips, rutabagas, carrots, and, although not strictly root vegetables, squash and onions. Shallots or wedges of red onion add extra color and flavor, and whole, unpeeled garlic cloves are also tasty.

prepare 15 minutes
cook 50 minutes–1 hour
serves 4–6

roasted root vegetables

ingredients

3 parsnips, cut into 2-inch/5-cm chunks

4 baby turnips, quartered

3 carrots, cut into 2-inch/5-cm chunks

1 lb/450 g butternut squash, peeled and cut into 2-inch/5-cm chunks

1 lb/450 g sweet potatoes, peeled and cut into 2-inch/5-cm chunks

2 garlic cloves, finely chopped

2 tbsp chopped fresh rosemary

2 tbsp chopped fresh thyme

2 tsp chopped fresh sage

3 tbsp olive oil

salt and pepper

2 tbsp chopped fresh mixed herbs, such as parsley, thyme, and mint, to garnish

one Preheat the oven to 425°F/220°C.

two Arrange all the vegetables in a single layer in a large roasting pan. Sprinkle over the garlic and the herbs. Pour over the oil and season well with salt and pepper.

three Toss all the ingredients together until they are well mixed and coated with the oil (you can let them marinate at this stage to allow the flavors to be absorbed).

four Roast the vegetables at the top of the oven for 50 minutes–1 hour until they are cooked and nicely browned. Turn the vegetables over halfway through the cooking time.

five Serve with a good handful of fresh herbs sprinkled on top and a final seasoning of salt and pepper to taste.

Ketchup has its place, but nothing compares with this homemade sauce, served with freshly cooked steaks or burgers. It is the perfect way to use up a glut of summer tomatoes, and will store well (see Cook's Tip).

prepare 10 minutes
cook 35 minutes
makes 500 ml/18 fl oz

homemade tomato sauce

ingredients

1 tbsp butter
2 tbsp olive oil
1 onion, chopped
1 garlic clove, finely chopped
14 oz/400 g canned tomatoes or
   1 lb/450 g fresh tomatoes, peeled
1 tbsp tomato paste
generous ⅓ cup red wine
⅔ cup vegetable stock
½ tsp sugar
1 bay leaf
salt and pepper

cook's tip

This sauce can be stored in an airtight container in the refrigerator for up to 4–5 days, or kept frozen for up to 3 months.

one Melt the butter with the oil in a large pan over medium heat, add the onion and garlic, and cook, stirring frequently, for 5 minutes, or until the onion has softened and is beginning to brown.

two Add all the remaining ingredients to the pan and season to taste with salt and pepper. Bring to a boil, then reduce the heat to low and let simmer, uncovered and stirring occasionally, for 30 minutes, or until the sauce has thickened.

three Remove and discard the bay leaf, pour the sauce into a food processor or blender, and process until smooth. Alternatively, using the back of a wooden spoon, push the sauce through a nylon strainer into a bowl.

four If serving immediately, reheat the sauce gently in a pan. Alternatively, store and reheat before serving.

This is the most famous southwestern salsa. Its name translates as "rooster's beak," so-called, allegedly, because it was traditionally eaten between the thumb and index finger, pecking-style. This fiery salsa is especially good with tortilla dishes, such as Chorizo and Cheese Quesadillas and Spinach and Mushroom Chimichangas.

prepare 10 minutes, plus 30 minutes' chilling
cook no cooking
serves 4–6

pico de gallo salsa

ingredients

3 large ripe tomatoes

½ red onion, finely chopped

1 large fresh green chili, such as jalapeño, seeded and finely chopped

2 tbsp chopped fresh cilantro

juice of 1 lime, or to taste

salt and pepper

one Halve the tomatoes, scoop out and discard the seeds, and dice the flesh. Place the flesh in a large, nonmetallic bowl.

two Add the onion, chili, chopped cilantro, and lime juice. Season to taste with salt and pepper and stir gently to combine.

three Cover and let chill in the refrigerator for at least 30 minutes to allow the flavors to develop before serving.

This is a relish you can rustle up reasonably quickly. Made in a small quantity, you only need to wait for it to cool before serving, rather than preserving it and letting it mature. It is an excellent accompaniment to Chili-Shrimp Tacos.

prepare 10 minutes, plus 2 hours' cooling
cook 15 minutes
serves 6–8

broiled bell pepper relish

ingredients

1 each of yellow, red, and green bell peppers
1 tbsp extra virgin olive oil
½ tsp brown sugar
1 tsp balsamic vinegar
¼ tsp salt
¼ tsp paprika

one Preheat the broiler to medium. Put the bell peppers onto a broiler rack and cook, turning frequently, for 15 minutes, or until the skins are charred all over.

two Transfer the bell peppers to a bowl, immediately cover with a clean, damp dish towel, and leave for at least 2 hours, or overnight, until cold.

three When the bell peppers are cold, hold them over a clean bowl to collect the juices and peel off the skin. Remove and discard the stem, core, and seeds and finely dice the flesh.

four Add the diced bell peppers to the juices in the bowl, then add the oil, sugar, vinegar, salt, and paprika. Stir together until well mixed and serve, or store in an airtight container in the refrigerator for up to 4–5 days.

cook's tip

This recipe uses a selection of different-colored bell peppers, but this isn't essential—it just makes the preserve look more colorful. You could use all of one color or two colors if preferred.

Along with Hush Puppies, this is an essential side dish for a pan-fried catfish meal. Some recipes are made with mayonnaise, but this version is less cloying. It also goes well with Barbecue Rack of Ribs and Southern Fried Chicken.

prepare 15 minutes,
plus 1 hour's chilling
cook no cooking
serves 4–6

coleslaw

ingredients

8 oz/225 g white cabbage, cored
   and grated
8 oz/225 g carrots, grated
4 tbsp superfine sugar
3 tbsp cider vinegar
½ cup heavy cream
2 pickled green or red bell peppers,
   drained and thinly sliced (optional)
4 tbsp finely chopped fresh parsley
salt and pepper

one Combine the cabbage, carrots, sugar, vinegar, a large pinch of salt, and pepper to taste in a large bowl, tossing the ingredients together. Cover and let chill for 1 hour.

two Lightly whip the cream, then gently stir in with the pickled bell peppers, if using, and the parsley. Taste and add extra sugar, vinegar, or salt, if desired. Serve immediately or cover and let chill until required.

did you know?

Coleslaw isn't exclusive to the South—
every region of America has a version
of this creamy, crunchy salad—but it
has been a part of southern culinary
history since European settlers arrived.
One of the earliest southern versions is
recorded in the Kentucky Housewife,
published by Lettice Bryan in 1839.

Making a good Guacamole requires using high quality, ripe avocados. Mashing rather than puréeing gives control over the texture. This relish teams well with sour cream and salsa in tortilla-based dishes, such as Chorizo and Cheese Quesadillas, Chicken Fajitas, and Spinach and Mushroom Chimichangas.

prepare 15 minutes
cook no cooking
serves 4

guacamole

ingredients

2 large, ripe avocados

1 lime

2 tsp olive oil

½ onion, finely chopped

1 fresh green chili, such as poblano,
 seeded and finely chopped

1 garlic clove, crushed

¼ tsp ground cumin

1 tbsp chopped fresh cilantro, plus extra
 to garnish (optional)

salt and pepper

one Cut each avocado in half lengthwise and twist the 2 halves in opposite directions to separate. Stab the pit of each avocado with the point of a sharp knife and lift out.

two Peel, then coarsely chop the avocado halves and place in a nonmetallic bowl. Squeeze over the juice of 1 lime and add the oil.

three Mash the avocados with a fork until the desired consistency—either chunky or smooth—is reached. Blend in the onion, chili, garlic, cumin, and chopped cilantro, then season to taste with salt and pepper.

four Transfer to a serving dish and serve immediately, to avoid discoloration, sprinkled with extra chopped cilantro, if liked.

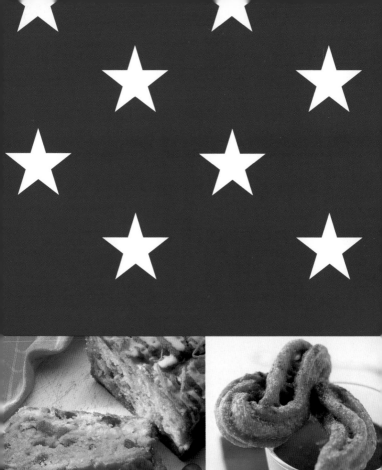

cakes and desserts

The addition of chopped nuts, candied peel, fresh orange juice, and dried cranberries makes this a rich, moist tea bread. The drizzled frosting and sprinkled orange rind add a decorative touch.

prepare 45 minutes
cook 1 hour
serves 8

banana and cranberry loaf

ingredients

butter, for greasing

1 ½ cups self-rising flour

½ tsp baking powder

⅔ cup brown sugar

2 bananas, mashed

⅓ cup chopped candied peel

¼ cup chopped mixed nuts

½ cup dried cranberries

5–6 tbsp orange juice

2 eggs, beaten

⅔ cup sunflower-seed or corn oil

¾ cup confectioners' sugar, sifted

grated rind of 1 orange

cook's tip

This tea bread will keep for a couple of days. Wrap it carefully and store in a cool, dry place.

one Preheat the oven to 350°F/180°C. Grease a 2 lb/900 g loaf pan and line the base with parchment paper.

two Sift the flour and baking powder into a mixing bowl. Stir in the brown sugar, bananas, chopped candied peel, nuts, and dried cranberries.

three Stir the orange juice, eggs, and oil together until well combined. Add the mixture to the dry ingredients and mix until thoroughly blended. Spoon the mixture into the prepared loaf pan and smooth the top.

four Bake in the oven for about 1 hour until firm to the touch or until a toothpick inserted into the center of the loaf comes out clean. Turn out the loaf and set aside on a cooling rack.

five Mix the confectioners' sugar with a little water and drizzle the frosting over the loaf. Sprinkle the orange rind over the top. Let the frosting set before slicing.

The pumpkin paste in this loaf makes it beautifully moist. It is delicious
eaten at any time of the day.

prepare 1½ hours
cook 2 hours 10 minutes
serves 6

pumpkin loaf

ingredients

vegetable oil, for greasing

1 lb/450 g pumpkin flesh

½ cup butter, softened, plus
    extra for greasing

¾ cup superfine sugar

2 eggs, lightly beaten

generous 1½ cups all-purpose flour

1½ tsp baking powder

½ tsp salt

1 tsp ground allspice

2 tbsp pumpkin seeds

one Preheat the oven to 400°F/200°C. Grease a 2-lb/900-g loaf pan with oil.

two Chop the pumpkin into large pieces and wrap in buttered foil. Cook in the oven for
30–40 minutes until they are tender. Reduce the oven temperature to 325°F/160°C. Let the
pumpkin cool completely before mashing well to make a thick paste.

three In a bowl, cream the butter and sugar together until light and fluffy. Add the beaten
eggs, a little at a time. Stir in the pumpkin paste then sift in the flour, baking powder, salt,
and allspice.

four Fold the pumpkin seeds gently through the mixture in a figure-eight movement. Spoon
the mixture into the prepared loaf pan. Bake in the oven for about 1¼–1½ hours or until a
skewer inserted into the center of the loaf comes out clean.

five Transfer the loaf to a cooling rack to cool, then serve, sliced and buttered, if wished.

cook's tip

To ensure that the pumpkin paste is
dry, place it in a pan over medium
heat for a few minutes, stirring
frequently, until it is thick.

A no-fuss cookie to enjoy with a cup of coffee. They are very easy-to-make and they can be stored in airtight containers for several days.

prepare 10 minutes
cook 15 minutes
makes 30

classic oatmeal cookies

ingredients

¾ cup butter or margarine,
  plus extra for greasing
1⅓ cups packed raw sugar
1 egg
4 tbsp water
1 tsp vanilla extract
4⅓ cups rolled oats
1 cup all-purpose flour
1 tsp salt
½ tsp baking soda

one Preheat the oven to 350°F/180°C and grease a large baking sheet.

two Cream the butter and sugar together in a large mixing bowl or with an electric mixer. Beat in the egg, water, and vanilla extract until the mixture is smooth.

three In a separate bowl, mix the oats, flour, salt, and baking soda. Gradually stir the oat mixture into the butter mixture until thoroughly combined.

four Put 30 rounded tablespoonfuls of cookie dough onto the greased baking sheet, making sure they are well spaced. Transfer to the oven and bake for 15 minutes, or until the cookies are golden brown.

five Remove the cookies from the oven and place on a cooling rack to cool before serving.

No chocolate-loving cook's repertoire would be complete without a chocolate chip cookie recipe. This recipe can be used to make several different varieties (see Variations).

prepare 35 minutes
cook 10–12 minutes
makes 18

chocolate chip cookies

ingredients

1½ cups all-purpose flour, sifted

1 tsp baking powder

½ cup soft margarine

scant ⅔ cup light brown sugar

¼ cup superfine sugar

½ tsp vanilla extract

1 egg

⅔ cup semisweet chocolate chips

one Preheat the oven to 375°F/190°C. Place all the ingredients in a large mixing bowl and beat until they are thoroughly combined.

two Lightly grease 2 cookie sheets. Place tablespoonfuls of the mixture onto the cookie sheets, spacing them well apart to allow for spreading during cooking.

three Bake in the oven for 10–12 minutes until the cookies are golden brown.

four Using a spatula, transfer the cookies to a cooling rack to cool completely before serving.

variations

For Choc and Nut Cookies, add ½ cup chopped hazelnuts to the basic mixture. For Double Choc Cookies, beat in 1½ oz/40 g melted semisweet chocolate. For White Chocolate Chip Cookies, use white chocolate chips instead of the semisweet chocolate chips.

Pecans and chocolate complement each other very successfully in this version of brownies. Dust with confectioner's sugar, if liked.

prepare 15 minutes
cook 40 minutes
makes 20

pecan brownies

ingredients

2½ oz/70 g semisweet chocolate
1 cup all-purpose flour
¾ tsp baking soda
¼ tsp baking powder
1 cup unsalted butter, plus extra
   for greasing

½ cup packed raw sugar
½ tsp almond extract
1 egg
½ cup pecans
1 tsp milk
confectioner's sugar, for dusting

one Preheat the oven to 350°F/180°C. Grease a large roasting pan and line it with parchment paper.

two Put the chocolate in a heatproof bowl over a pan of simmering water (a double boiler is ideal) and heat until it is melted. While the chocolate is melting, sift together the flour, baking soda, and baking powder in a large bowl.

three In a separate bowl, cream together the butter and sugar, then mix in the almond extract and the egg. Remove the chocolate from the heat and stir into the butter mixture. Chop the pecans finely, then add them to the bowl, along with the flour mixture and milk, and stir until well combined.

four Spoon the cookie dough into the lined roasting pan and level it. Transfer to the oven and cook for 30 minutes, or until firm to the touch (it should still be a little gooey in the middle). Remove from the oven and leave to cool completely. Remove from the roasting pan and cut into 20 squares. Dust with confectioner's sugar and serve.

This southwestern-style doughnut looks rather more appealing than its traditional relative, since the dough is piped into lengths, which twist into a variety of interesting shapes when deep-fried. Churros go equally well with a cup of hot chocolate or a coffee.

prepare 25 minutes, plus 3 minutes' cooling
cook 20 minutes
serves 4

churros

ingredients

1 cup water

7 tbsp butter or shortening, diced

2 tbsp brown sugar

finely grated rind of 1 small orange (optional)

pinch of salt

1⅛ cups all-purpose flour, sifted

1 tsp ground cinnamon, plus extra for dusting

1 tsp vanilla extract

2 eggs

vegetable oil, for deep-frying

superfine sugar, for dusting

one Heat the water, butter, brown sugar, orange rind, if using, and salt in a heavy-bottom pan over medium heat until the butter has melted.

two Add the flour, all at once, the cinnamon, and vanilla extract, then remove the pan from the heat and beat rapidly until the mixture pulls away from the side of the pan.

three Let cool slightly, then beat in the eggs, one at a time, beating well after each addition, until the mixture is thick and smooth. Spoon into a pastry bag fitted with a wide star tip.

four Heat the oil for deep-frying in a deep-fryer or deep pan to 350–375°F/180–190°C, or until a cube of bread browns in 30 seconds. Pipe 5-inch/13-cm lengths about 3 inches/7.5 cm apart into the oil. Deep-fry for 4 minutes, or until golden brown. Remove with a slotted spoon and drain on paper towels.

five Dust the churros with superfine sugar and cinnamon and serve either hot from the pan or cooled to room temperature.

These sweet empanadas have a creamy, fruity filling and a hint of crunchy nut. You could use apricots or mangoes in place of the peaches, adding some extra slices of fruit to decorate. Serve as a snack or a dessert.

peach and pecan empanadas

ingredients

all-purpose flour, for dusting

12 oz/350 g ready-made puff pastry,
   thawed if frozen

3 fresh peaches

²⁄₃ cup sour cream

4 tbsp brown sugar

4 tbsp pecan halves, toasted and
   finely chopped

beaten egg, to glaze

superfine sugar, for sprinkling

one Preheat the oven to 400°F/200°C. Roll out the pastry on a lightly floured counter. Using a 6-inch/15-cm saucer as a guide, cut out 8 circles.

two Cut a small cross in the stem end of each peach. Lower them into a pan of boiling water and let stand for 10–30 seconds, depending on ripeness. Drain and cool under cold running water to prevent further cooking. Peel using a small knife.

three Place a spoonful of sour cream on the center of a pastry circle and top with a few peach slices. Sprinkle over a little brown sugar and some nuts. Brush each edge with a little beaten egg, fold the pastry over the filling, and press the edges together to seal. Crimp the edges with a fork and prick the tops.

four Place on a baking sheet, brush with beaten egg, and sprinkle with superfine sugar. Bake in the oven for 20 minutes, or until they turn golden brown. Serve warm.

This classic cherry pie can be made at any time of the year, but if you are using fresh cherries then its exact appearance may vary according to the types of cherry that are in season.

prepare 40 minutes, plus 30 minutes' chilling
cook 55 minutes
serves 6

latticed cherry pie

ingredients

Pie dough

1 cup all-purpose flour, plus extra
  for dusting

¼ tsp baking powder

½ tsp allspice

½ tsp salt

¼ cup superfine sugar

4 tbsp cold unsalted butter, diced,

plus extra for greasing

water, for sealing

1 beaten egg, plus extra for glazing

Filling

2 lb/900 g pitted fresh or canned
  cherries, drained

¾ cup granulated sugar

½ tsp almond extract

2 tsp cherry brandy

¼ tsp allspice

2 tbsp cornstarch

2 tbsp water

2 tbsp cold unsalted butter, diced

freshly whipped cream or ice cream,
  to serve

one To make the pie dough, sift the flour and baking powder into a large bowl. Stir in the allspice, salt, and sugar. Using your fingertips, rub in the butter until the mixture resembles fine bread crumbs, then make a well in the center. Pour the beaten egg into the well. Mix with a wooden spoon, then shape the mixture into a dough. Cut the dough in half and use your hands to roll each half into a ball. Wrap the dough and let chill in the refrigerator for 30 minutes.

two Preheat the oven to 425°F/220°C. Grease a 9-inch/23-cm round pie dish with butter. Roll out the dough into 2 circles, each 12 inches/30 cm in diameter. Use one to line the pie dish. Trim the edge, leaving an overhang of ½ inch/1 cm.

three To make the filling, place half the cherries and all the sugar in a large pan. Bring to a simmer over low heat, stirring, for 5 minutes, or until the sugar has melted. Stir in the almond extract, cherry brandy, and allspice. In a separate bowl, mix the cornstarch and water to form a paste. Remove the pan from the heat, stir in the cornstarch, then return to the heat and stir constantly until the mixture boils and thickens. Let cool a little. Stir in the remaining cherries, pour into the pastry shell, then dot with the butter.

four Cut the dough circle into long strips ½-inch/1-cm wide. Lay strips evenly across the top of the filling in the same direction, folding back every other strip. Now lay more strips crosswise over the original strips, folding back every other strip each time you add another crosswise strip, to form a lattice. Trim off the ends and seal the edges with water. Use your fingers to crimp around the rim, then brush the top with beaten egg. Cover with foil, then bake for 30 minutes. Remove from the oven, discard the foil, then return the pie to the oven for an additional 15 minutes, or until cooked and golden. Serve warm with freshly whipped cream or ice cream.

variation

If you prefer, you can use the other circle of dough whole to cover the pie. Trim the edge, seal with water, and crimp around the rim, then brush with beaten egg. Make two slits in the center with a sharp knife to let out the steam.

This apple pie has a double crust and is delicious either hot or cold.
The apples can be flavored with other spices or grated citrus rind.

prepare 30 minutes,
plus 30 minutes' chilling
cook 50 minutes
serves 6

traditional apple pie

ingredients

Pie dough

2½ cups all-purpose flour

pinch of salt

7 tbsp butter or margarine, diced

7 tbsp lard or vegetable shortening,
 diced

about 6 tbsp cold water

beaten egg or milk, for glazing

Filling

1 lb 10 oz–2 lb 4 oz/750 g–1 kg
 baking apples

scant ⅔ cup packed brown or superfine
 sugar, plus extra for sprinkling

½–1 tsp ground cinnamon, allspice,
 or ground ginger

1–2 tbsp water (optional)

one To make the pie dough, sift the flour and salt into a large bowl. Add the butter and lard
and rub in with the fingertips until the mixture resembles fine bread crumbs. Add the water
and gather the mixture together into a dough. Wrap the dough and let chill in the refrigerator
for 30 minutes.

two Preheat the oven to 425°F/220°C. Roll out almost two-thirds of the pie dough thinly and
use to line a deep 9-inch/23-cm pie plate or pie pan.

three Peel, core, and slice the apples, then mix with the sugar and spice and pack into the
pastry shell; the filling can come up above the rim. Add the water if needed, particularly if the
apples are a dry variety.

four Roll out the remaining pie dough to form a lid. Dampen the edges of the pie rim with
water and position the lid, pressing the edges firmly together. Trim and crimp the edges.

five Use the trimmings to cut out leaves or other shapes to decorate the top of the pie;
dampen and attach. Glaze the top of the pie with beaten egg or milk, make 1–2 slits in the
top, and place the pie on a baking sheet.

six Bake in the oven for 20 minutes, then reduce the temperature to 350°F/180°C and bake
for a further 30 minutes, or until the pastry is a light golden brown. Serve hot or cold,
sprinkled with sugar.

Serve slices of this pie and see if guests can guess the main ingredient—few people will expect the humble sweet potato to be turned into such a rich, indulgent dessert.

prepare 30 minutes,
plus 1 hour's chilling
cook 1 hour
serves 8–10

sweet potato pie

ingredients

Pie dough

1¼ cups all-purpose flour, plus extra
for dusting

½ tsp salt

¼ tsp superfine sugar

1½ tbsp butter, diced

3 tbsp white vegetable fat, diced

2–2½ tbsp ice-cold water

Filling

1 lb 2 oz/500 g orange-fleshed
sweet potatoes, scrubbed

3 extra-large eggs, beaten

½ cup packed brown sugar

1½ cups canned evaporated milk

3 tbsp butter, melted

2 tsp vanilla extract

1 tsp ground cinnamon

1 tsp ground nutmeg or freshly
grated nutmeg

½ tsp salt

freshly whipped cream, to serve

one To make the pie dough, sift the flour, salt, and sugar into a bowl. Add the butter and white vegetable fat to the bowl and rub in with the fingertips until fine crumbs form. Sprinkle over 2 tablespoons of the water and mix with a fork until a soft dough forms. Add ½ tablespoon of water if the dough is too dry. Wrap in plastic wrap and chill for at least 1 hour.

two Meanwhile, bring a large pan of water to a boil over high heat. Add the sweet potatoes and cook for 15 minutes. Drain, then cool them under cold running water. When cool, peel, then mash. Put the sweet potatoes into a separate bowl and beat in the eggs and sugar until very smooth. Beat in the remaining ingredients, then set aside until required.

three When ready to bake, preheat the oven to 425°F/220°C. Roll out the dough on a lightly floured counter into a thin 11-inch/28-cm circle and use to line a 9-inch/23-cm pie plate, about 1½ inches/4 cm deep. Trim off the excess dough and press the floured tines of a fork around the edge.

four Prick the base of the pastry shell all over with the fork and place crumpled kitchen foil in the center. Bake in the oven for 12 minutes, or until lightly golden.

five Remove the pastry shell from the oven, take out the foil, pour the filling into the shell, and return to the oven for an additional 10 minutes. Reduce the oven temperature to 325°F/160°C and bake for a further 35 minutes, or until a knife inserted into the center comes out clean. Let cool on a cooling rack. Serve warm or at room temperature with whipped cream.

Pumpkins have long been a staple of cooking in North America, with the fruit being used by both Native Americans and by later settlers, for whom it became a Thanksgiving favorite in New England.

prepare 30 minutes, plus 1 hour's cooling and chilling
cook 2 hours 20 minutes
serves 6

sweet pumpkin pie

ingredients

4 lb/1.8 kg sweet pumpkin

4 tbsp cold unsalted butter, diced, plus extra for greasing

1 cup all-purpose flour, plus extra for dusting

¼ tsp baking powder

1½ tsp ground cinnamon

¾ tsp ground nutmeg

¾ tsp ground cloves

1 tsp salt

¼ cup superfine sugar

3 eggs

1¾ cups sweetened condensed milk

½ tsp vanilla extract

1 tbsp raw sugar

Streusel topping

2 tbsp all-purpose flour

4 tbsp raw sugar

1 tsp ground cinnamon

2 tbsp cold unsalted butter, diced

generous ⅔ cup shelled pecans, chopped

generous ⅔ cup shelled walnuts, chopped

one Preheat the oven to 375°F/190°C. Quarter the pumpkin, remove the seeds, and set aside for roasting (see Cook's Tip). Remove and discard the stem and stringy insides. Place the pumpkin quarters, face down, in a shallow roasting pan and cover with foil. Bake in the oven for 1½ hours, then remove from the oven and let cool. Scoop out the flesh and mash with a potato masher or purée it in a food processor. Drain away any excess liquid. Cover with plastic wrap and let chill until ready to use. It will keep for 3 days (or several months in a freezer).

two To make the pie dough, first grease a 9-inch/23-cm round pie dish with butter. Sift the flour and baking powder into a large bowl. Stir in the spices and the superfine sugar. Rub in the butter with the fingertips until the mixture resembles fine bread crumbs, then make a well in the center. Lightly beat 1 egg and pour it into the well. Mix together with a wooden spoon, then use your hands to shape the dough into a ball. Place it on a clean counter lightly dusted with flour, and roll out to a circle large enough to line the pie dish. Use it to line the dish, then trim the edge. Cover the dish with plastic wrap and let chill in the refrigerator for 30 minutes.

three Preheat the oven to 425°F/220°C. To make the filling, place the pumpkin purée in a large bowl, then stir in the condensed milk and remaining eggs. Add the remaining spices and salt, then stir in the vanilla extract and raw sugar. Pour into the pastry shell and bake in the oven for 15 minutes.

four Meanwhile, make the topping. Combine the flour, sugar, and cinnamon in a bowl, rub in the butter until crumbly, then stir in the nuts. Remove the pie from the oven and reduce the heat to 350°F/180°C. Sprinkle the topping over the pie, then bake for an additional 35 minutes. Remove from the oven and serve hot or cold.

cook's tip

To roast pumpkin seeds, soak them in salt water overnight, then drain. Spread them out on a greased baking sheet. Sprinkle over a little salt for extra flavor. Bake in a preheated oven at 350°F/180°C for 20 minutes.

Maple syrup and pecans give a wonderful flavor to the toffee filling in these little tarts. Serve on their own, or with a little whipped cream for an extra-indulgent treat.

prepare 20 minutes, plus 30 minutes' chilling
cook 17–23 minutes
makes 12

maple pecan tarts

ingredients

Pie dough

1¼ cups all-purpose flour, plus extra
    for dusting
7 tbsp butter
¼ cup golden superfine sugar
2 egg yolks

Filling

2 tbsp maple syrup
⅔ cup heavy cream
generous ½ cup golden superfine sugar
pinch of cream of tartar
6 tbsp water
1 cup pecans plus 14 pecan halves,
    to decorate

one To make the pie dough, sift the flour into a mixing bowl and rub in the butter to form fine crumbs. Add the sugar and egg yolks, and mix to form a soft dough. Wrap and chill in the refrigerator for 30 minutes.

two Preheat the oven to 400°F/200°C. On a floured work counter, roll out the pie dough thinly, cut out 12 circles, and use to line 12 tartlet pans. Prick the bottoms and press a piece of foil into each tart shell. Bake in the oven for 10–15 minutes until light golden. Remove the foil and bake for an additional 2–3 minutes. Let cool on a cooling rack.

three To make the filling, mix half the maple syrup and half the cream in a bowl. Put the sugar, cream of tartar, and water in a pan and heat gently until the sugar dissolves. Bring to a boil and boil until light golden. Remove the pan from the heat and stir in the maple syrup and cream mixture.

four Return the pan to the heat and cook to the soft ball stage (240°F/116°C): that is, when a little of the mixture dropped into a bowl of cold water forms a soft ball. Stir in the remaining cream and leave until warm. Brush the remaining maple syrup over the edges of the tarts. Put the pecans in the pastry shells and spoon in the maple syrup mixture. Top each one with a pecan. Let cool before serving.

The thought of a "mud pie" might not be appealing, but this chilled chocolate pie with pecans is anything but unappetizing. It is so rich that thin slices will suffice for most guests.

prepare 20 minutes, plus 20 minutes' cooling and chilling
cook 30 minutes
serves 12–14

mississippi mud pie

ingredients

Crumb crust

5 oz/140 g graham crackers
½ cup pecans, finely chopped
1 tbsp light brown sugar
½ tsp ground cinnamon
6 tbsp butter, melted

Filling

1 cup butter or margarine, plus extra for greasing
6 oz/175 g semisweet chocolate, chopped
½ cup corn syrup
4 large eggs, beaten
½ cup pecans, finely chopped
whipped cream, to serve

one Preheat the oven to 350°F/180°C. Lightly grease a 9-inch/23-cm springform or loose-bottom cake pan.

two To make the crumb crust, put the graham crackers, pecans, sugar, and cinnamon into a food processor and process until fine crumbs form—do not overprocess to a powder. Add the melted butter and process again until moistened.

three Tip the crumb mixture into the cake pan and press over the bottom and about 1½ inches/4 cm up the side of the pan. Cover the pan and let chill while making the filling.

four To make the filling, put the butter, chocolate, and corn syrup into a pan over low heat and stir until melted and blended. Let cool, then beat in the eggs and pecans.

five Pour the filling into the chilled crumb crust and smooth the surface. Bake in the oven for 30 minutes, or until just set but still soft in the center. Let cool on a cooling rack. Serve at room temperature or chilled with whipped cream.

did you know?

This rich chocolate pie gets its name from the dark brown color of the filling—said to resemble the rich mud along the banks of the Mississippi.

Tart and creamy, this classic American pie is ideal for summer entertaining. Commercial key lime pies have green food coloring added, but this recipe is undoctored and so has a pale cream color.

prepare 20 minut
plus 2½ hours' cool
and chill
cook 20 minut
serves

key lime pie

ingredients

Crumb crust

6 oz/175 g graham crackers or
gingersnap cookies
2 tbsp superfine sugar
½ tsp ground cinnamon
6 tbsp butter, melted

Filling

1¾ cups canned sweetened
condensed milk
½ cup freshly squeezed lime juice
finely grated rind of 3 limes
4 large egg yolks
freshly whipped cream, to serve

one Preheat the oven to 325°F/160°C. Lightly grease a 9-inch/23-cm pie plate, about 1½-inches/4-cm deep.

two To make the crumb crust, put the graham crackers, sugar, and cinnamon into a food processor and process until fine crumbs form—do not overprocess to a powder. Add the melted butter and process again until moistened.

three Tip the crumb mixture into the pie plate and press over the bottom and up the side. Place the pie plate on a baking sheet and bake in the oven for 5 minutes.

four Meanwhile, beat the condensed milk, lime juice, lime rind, and egg yolks together in a bowl until well blended.

five Remove the crumb crust from the oven, pour the filling into the crumb crust, and spread out to the edge. Return to the oven for an additional 15 minutes, or until the filling is set around the edge but still wobbly in the center. Let cool completely on a cooling rack, then cover and let chill for at least 2 hours. Serve with dollops of whipped cream.

did you know

*This pie dates from the late 18...
after canned condensed milk beca...
available—a welcome developm...
in the remote Florida Keys, wi...
fresh milk was a luxury. Key li...
aren't commercially grown elsewh...
and their season is short, so ordi...
limes are most frequently use...
this all-American favo...*

Summertime in Georgia means one thing—peaches, peaches, and more peaches. This old-fashioned baked dessert with its "cobblestone" topping is a traditional way to take advantage of the seasonal glut.

prepare 20 minute
cook 35 minute
serves 4-

peach cobbler

ingredients

6 peaches, peeled and sliced
  (see Cook's Tip)
4 tbsp superfine sugar
½ tbsp lemon juice
1½ tsp cornstarch
½ tsp almond or vanilla extract
vanilla or butter pecan ice cream,
  to serve

Cobbler topping

1¼ cups all-purpose flour
generous ½ cup superfine sugar
1½ tsp baking powder
½ tsp salt
6 tbsp butter, diced
1 egg
5–6 tbsp milk

one Preheat the oven to 425°F/220°C. Put the peaches into a 9-inch/23-cm square ovenproof dish that is also suitable for serving. Add the sugar, lemon juice, cornstarch, and almond extract and toss together. Bake the peaches in the oven for 20 minutes.

two Meanwhile, to make the topping, sift the flour, all but 2 tablespoons of the sugar, the baking powder, and salt into a bowl. Rub in the butter with the fingertips until fine crumbs form. Combine the egg and 5 tablespoons of the milk in a pitcher and mix into the dry ingredients with a fork until a soft, sticky dough forms. If the dough seems dry, stir in the extra tablespoon of milk.

three Reduce the oven temperature to 400°F/200°C. Remove the peaches from the oven and drop spoonfuls of the topping over the surface, without smoothing. Sprinkle with the remaining sugar, return to the oven, and bake for an additional 15 minutes, or until the topping is golden brown and firm—the topping will spread as it cooks. Serve hot or at room temperature with ice cream on the side.

cook's ti

To peel the peaches, cut a sma
  cross in the stem end of each
peach. Lower them into a pan
  boiling water and let stand
    10–30 seconds, depending
ripeness. Drain and cool under c
  running water to prevent furth
  cooking. Peel using a small kn

As the batter sits, it tends to thicken up and can make the pancakes very doughy. If the mixture becomes too thick while you are cooking the pancakes, add a little extra milk before continuing.

prepare 5 minutes
cook 20 minutes
serves 4–6
makes 18

apple pancakes with maple syrup butter

ingredients

scant 1½ cups self-rising flour, sifted

½ cup superfine sugar

1 tsp ground cinnamon

1 egg

scant 1 cup milk

2 apples, peeled and grated

1 tbsp butter

strawberries, to serve

Maple syrup butter

7 tbsp butter, softened

3 tbsp maple syrup

one Mix the flour, sugar, and cinnamon together in a bowl and make a well in the center. Beat the egg and the milk together and pour into the well. Using a wooden spoon, gently incorporate the dry ingredients into the liquid until well combined, then stir in the grated apple.

two Heat the butter in a large nonstick skillet over low heat until melted and bubbling. Add tablespoons of the pancake mixture to form 3½-inch/9-cm circles. Cook each pancake for about 1 minute, or until it starts to bubble lightly on the top and looks set, then flip it over and cook the other side for 30 seconds, or until cooked through. The pancakes should be golden brown; if not, increase the heat a little. Remove from the skillet and keep warm. Repeat the process until all of the pancake batter has been used up (it is not necessary to add extra butter).

three To make the maple syrup butter, melt the butter with the maple syrup in a pan over low heat and stir until combined. To serve, place the pancakes on serving dishes and spoon over the flavored butter. Serve warm with some ripe strawberries for added color and flavor.

For many southern families, the Christmas Day feast isn't complete without this coconut and orange salad, served in the best cut-glass bowl. And for busy cooks, ambrosia is also ideal for entertaining at any time of the year as it can be assembled a day ahead.

prepare 45 minutes, plus 2 hours' chilling
cook no cooking
serves 4–6

ambrosia

ingredients

1 fresh coconut

3 large oranges

½ tbsp freshly squeezed lemon juice

confectioners' sugar, to taste (optional)

one To prepare the coconut, use a hammer and nail or screw to puncture the soft eyes at the top. Drain the coconut liquid into a bowl. Use the hammer to gently tap the coconut shell all round until it cracks and splits on its own. Cut the coconut meat away from the hard shell, then peel off and discard the thin brown membrane. Use a food processor or hand grater to grate 2 cups of the coconut meat, then set aside.

two Peel the oranges over a bowl to catch the juices, carefully removing all the bitter white pith. Cut the oranges into ¼-inch/5-mm slices, removing and discarding the seeds.

three Put the coconut, orange slices, reserved orange juice, and the lemon juice into a large glass serving bowl and toss together. Taste and sift over a little confectioners' sugar if the orange juice is not sweet enough, then toss again.

four Cover and let chill for at least 2 hours, tossing the ingredients together frequently and just before serving.

did you know?

Southerners were so fond of this ethereal combination that they gave it the title "ambrosia," from Greek and Roman mythology—ambrosia was the food that the gods ate to preserve their immortality. It is said that the dish originated from the time when crates of fresh oranges and/or coconuts were common Christmas gifts.

"Butter pecan" is one of America's favorite ice-cream flavors. This recipe from Georgia illustrates why—it is ultra-rich and sweet. Serve after a light main course, or scoop into cones for a summer treat.

prepare 30 minutes, plus 2–6 hours' cooling, chilling, and freezing
cook no cooking
serves 8–10

butter pecan ice cream

ingredients

1½ cups heavy cream
¾ cup milk
6 egg yolks
½ cup superfine sugar
½ cup cooled clarified butter (see Cook's Tip), diced
1½ cups coarsely chopped pecans

cook's tip

For a smooth finish, it is important to use clarified butter, which has had the milk solids removed. To make ½ cup, melt ¾ cup of butter in a pan over low heat. Remove from the heat and let the milk solids sink to the bottom. Skim off the foam, then carefully pour off the bright yellow clarified butter.

one Bring ½ cup of the cream and all the milk to a boil in a pan over medium-high heat. Remove the pan from the heat and let the mixture cool completely. Pour into a bowl, cover, and let chill for 30 minutes.

two Using an electric mixer on high speed, beat the egg yolks with 4 tablespoons of the sugar until pale and thick enough to hold a ribbon on the surface when the beaters are lifted. Set aside.

three Combine the remaining cream and sugar in the rinsed-out pan and bring just to a boil. Pour about half the hot cream into the egg mixture, beating constantly, then pour all this mixture into the pan, stirring to blend both mixtures together. Heat just until small bubbles appear around the edge. Add the clarified butter and stir until it melts.

four Pour the mixture into a bowl and let cool completely, stirring occasionally. Pour in the chilled cream-and-milk mixture and stir until blended. Pour the mixture into an ice-cream maker and freeze according to the manufacturer's directions. When it is about three-quarters frozen, stir in the nuts. Alternatively, pour the mixture into a freezerproof container, cover, and freeze for 1 hour, or until partially frozen. Remove from the freezer and beat with a fork until smooth. Re-cover and return to the freezer. Repeat the freezing and beating process, then stir in the nuts, return to the freezer, and freeze for 1½–2 hours, or until firm. Serve in scoops.

Chocolate and chili are a classic southwestern combination in savory dishes, but can also be used together in sweet dishes. The chili just gives a warmth and richness to the chocolate. Reserve this rich dessert for serving after a middle-weight main course, such as the Salisbury Steak, Chili-Shrimp Tacos, or Chicken Fajitas.

prepare 15–25 minutes,
plus 15 minutes'–2 hours'
processing or freezing
cook 10 minutes
serves 4

chocolate chip and chili ice cream

ingredients

1 egg and 1 egg yolk
generous ¼ cup superfine sugar
5½ oz/150 g semisweet chocolate,
   finely chopped
scant 2½ cups milk
1 dried red chili, such as ancho
1 vanilla bean
scant 2½ cups heavy cream
scant 1 cup semisweet, milk, or white
   chocolate chips

one Place the egg, egg yolk, and sugar in a heatproof bowl set over a pan of simmering water. Beat until light and fluffy.

two Place the chopped chocolate, milk, chili, and vanilla bean in a separate pan and heat gently until the chocolate has dissolved and the milk is almost boiling. Pour onto the egg mixture, discarding the chili and vanilla bean, and beat well. Let cool.

three Lightly whip the cream in a separate bowl. Fold into the cold mixture with the chocolate chips. Transfer to an ice-cream machine and process for 15 minutes, or according to the manufacturer's instructions. Alternatively, transfer to a freezerproof container and freeze for 1 hour, or until partially frozen. Remove from the freezer, transfer to a bowl, and beat to break down the ice crystals. Freeze again for 30 minutes, then beat again. Freeze once more until firm.

four Transfer the ice cream to the refrigerator 15 minutes before serving. Serve in scoops.

When you want to chill out, literally, this ice-cold dessert will hit the spot. It couldn't be more elegant. To add a finishing touch, decorate with lime slices or twists, or finely pared strips of rind.

prepare 20 minutes, plus 2½ hours' chilling
cook 10 minutes
serves 4

guava, lime, and tequila sherbet

ingredients

scant 1 cup superfine sugar

scant 2 cups water

4 fresh ripe guavas or 8 canned
   guava halves

2 tbsp tequila

juice of ½ lime, or to taste

1 egg white

one Heat the sugar and water in a heavy-bottom pan over low heat until the sugar has dissolved. When the liquid turns clear, boil for 5 minutes, or until a thick syrup forms. Remove the pan from the heat and let cool.

two Cut the fresh guavas, if using, in half. Scoop out the flesh. Discard the seeds from the fresh or canned guava flesh. Transfer to a food processor or blender and process until smooth.

three Add the purée to the syrup with the tequila and lime juice to taste. Transfer the mixture to a freezerproof container and freeze for 1 hour, or until slushy.

four Remove from the freezer and process again until smooth. Return to the freezer and freeze until firm. Process again until smooth. With the motor still running, add the egg white through the feeder tube. Freeze until solid.

five Transfer the sherbet to the refrigerator 15 minutes before serving. Serve in scoops.

This flambéed dish, originally from Brennan's, one of the best-known restaurants in New Orleans, makes a spectacular end to any meal. It derives its name from Richard Foster, a friend of the owner. The cinnamon-flavored syrup can be made in advance, ready for the flaming finale.

prepare 10 minutes
cook 10 minutes
serves 4

bananas foster

ingredients

1 cup dark brown sugar

½ cup butter, diced

1 tsp ground cinnamon

4 firm bananas

4 scoops premium-quality vanilla
   ice cream

4 tbsp rum

1 tbsp bourbon

one Put the sugar, butter, and cinnamon into a large skillet over high heat and stir constantly until the sugar and butter melt. Cook, stirring constantly, for a further 3–4 minutes until a golden brown syrup forms.

two Cut the bananas in half lengthwise and slice into the syrup, then gently turn the slices until they are coated and heated through. Meanwhile, put a scoop of ice cream into each of 4 individual heatproof serving bowls.

three Heat the rum and bourbon in a long-handled ladle then ignite. Pour the flaming spirits into the banana mixture, then spoon the banana mixture over the ice cream and serve immediately.

did you know?

Although Bananas Foster is often served as a dessert, the recipe was devised in the 1950s as part of a "Breakfast at Brennan's" brunch promotion—a tradition that continues today with table-side flambéing. Bananas Foster has become so popular that it now appears on menus throughout the South, especially in Florida.

This silken dessert with its caramel topping is traditional in Mexico and is commonly known as "flan." The addition of chocolate makes it even more luxurious and tempting.

prepare 15 minutes,
plus 2 hours' cooling
and chilling
cook 1¼ hours
serves 4

mexican chocolate crème caramel

ingredients

generous ½ cup granulated sugar

4 tbsp water

2½ cups milk

2 oz/55 g semisweet chocolate, grated

4 eggs

2 tbsp superfine sugar

1 tsp vanilla extract

blueberries and raspberries, to decorate

variations

Decorate with some chocolate curls for a special occasion, or add some sliced banana for a comforting treat.

one Preheat the oven to 325°F/160°C. Place a 4-cup soufflé dish in the oven to heat.

two Place the granulated sugar and water in a heavy-bottom pan over low heat. Stir until the sugar has dissolved. Bring to a boil, without stirring, and boil until caramelized. Pour into the hot dish, tipping it to coat the bottom and sides. Let cool.

three Place the milk and grated chocolate in a separate pan and heat, stirring occasionally, until the chocolate has dissolved.

four Meanwhile, beat the eggs and superfine sugar together in a bowl with a wooden spoon. Gradually beat in the chocolate milk. Add the vanilla extract. Strain into the prepared dish.

five Stand the dish in a roasting pan and fill the pan with enough lukewarm water to come halfway up the sides of the dish. Bake in the oven for 1 hour, or until set. Let cool, then invert onto a serving plate. Let chill in the refrigerator before serving decorated with berries.

index